Philip De Carteret R.N.

Jersey's exceptional but forgotten explorer

Jane Ashelford

SEAFLOWER BOOKS
in partnership with Jersey Heritage

Published in 2020 by
SEAFLOWER BOOKS
in partnership with Jersey Heritage

www.ex-librisbooks.co.uk

Origination by Ex Libris Press

Printed and bound by CPI Group (UK) Ltd,
Croydon, CR0 4YY

ISBN 978-1-912020-87-4

Contents

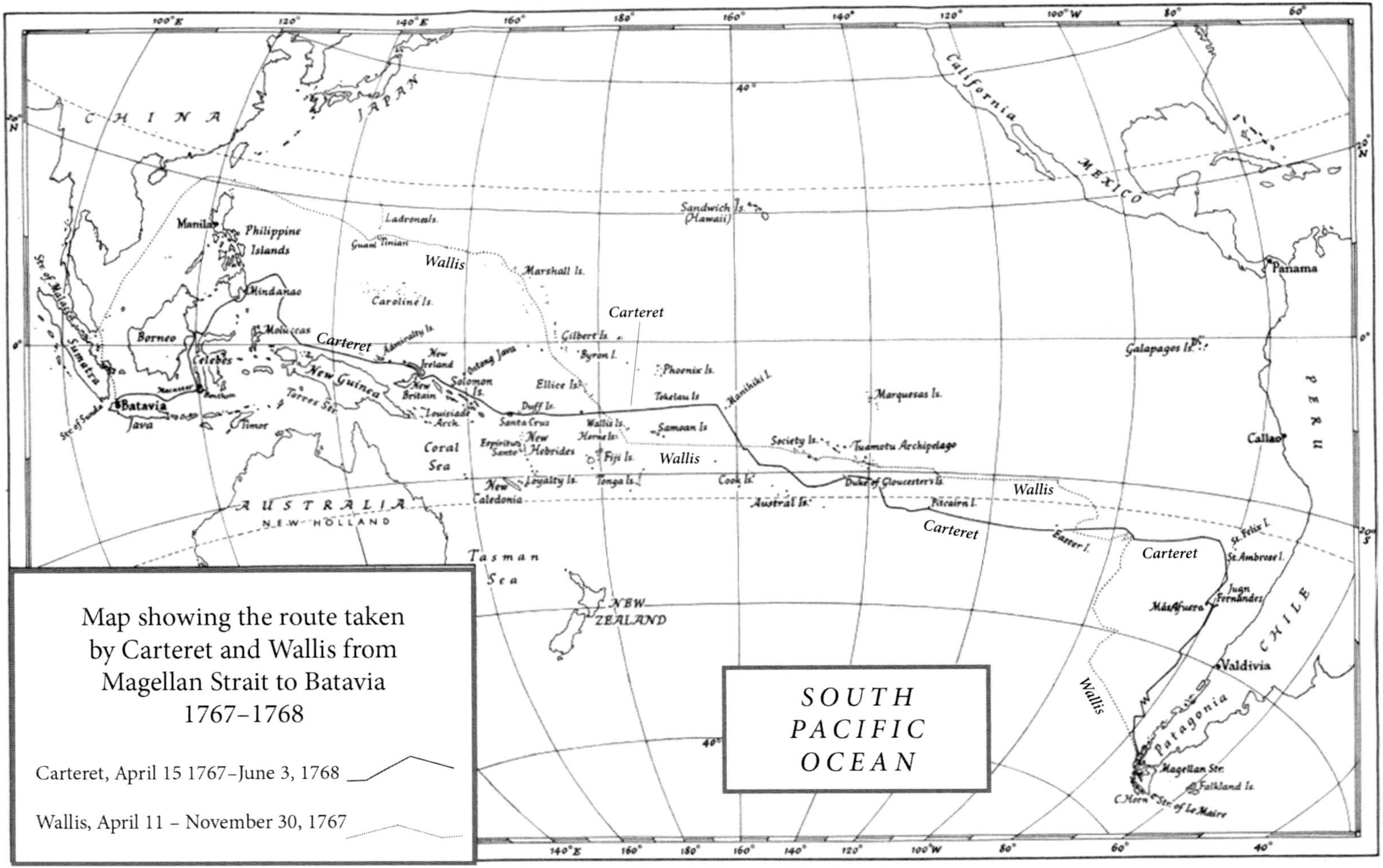

Map showing the route taken by Carteret and Wallis from Magellan Strait to Batavia 1767–1768

Introduction

At half past noon on Monday 20 February 1769 the Royal Navy ship *Swallow*[1] (see Plate 1) and the French Navy ship *Boudeuse*[2] came within hailing distance of each other just to the south-west of the Cape Verde Islands at Latitude 13° 10' N and Longitude 26° 37' West. Their last landfall had been the uninhabited Ascension Island where it was the custom for ships sailing back to Europe from India and the East to leave a message in a bottle noting the date of their arrival and departure. As it was too early in the season for a commercial ship to be sailing back to Europe, Commander Philip Carteret of the *Swallow* was not only 'greatly surprised' but very suspicious to encounter in the vast expanse of the South Atlantic Ocean a 'stranger calling me, and the Ship by our Names' and then finding out that the Commander of the ship was 'well acquainted with my voyage'.

The *Boudeuse,* under the command of Louis Antoine de Bougainville, had left Nantes on 15 November 1766 on the first French voyage of circumnavigation with two secret and diplomatically sensitive objectives: firstly, handing over the Falkland Islands, *Les Iles Malouines* – which the British laid claim to the Spanish and secondly, exploration of the Pacific Ocean in the hope of finding 'the great Unknown Southern Continent', thus enabling the French to establish a presence in that part of the world. It was the most scientific voyage to the South Seas, being the first to carry out astronomical observations of longitude, to study the zoology of the area and to make a systematic collection of botanical specimens. Under conditions of the greatest secrecy the Admiralty had also instructed two Royal Navy officers, Philip Carteret and Samuel Wallis, to explore the same area in the hope of finding 'a place of consequence in the South Seas'. The two Royal Navy ships, the *Dolphin* and the *Swallow*, left Plymouth on 21 August 1766 but were separated in stormy seas when they left the Straits of Magellan. When the *Dolphin* returned to England 17 months later it was assumed that the *Swallow* had foundered and been lost. In contrast to the *Boudeuse*, a new frigate of 550 tons with a crew of 11 officers and 203 men, the *Swallow* was a lumbering twenty year-old sloop which had left England with an inadequate crew of 86 men and was, in the opinion of Carteret, 'neither a fit Vesell, or properly fitted out for service in the South Seas'.

Carteret did not know that Bougainville had found evidence of *Swallow*'s arrival at New Ireland and Ascension Island. He was also unaware of the fact that, during his stay at the Cape of Good Hope in January 1769, Bougainville had found out what had happened to the *Dolphin* after its separation from the *Swallow* by reading reports published in the *Gazette de France* during June 1768. Despite strict instructions that he was 'neither to salute English vessels or to seek salutations from them' was determined to catch up with his fellow circumnavigator. When he finally sighted the British ship he could not believe how they had survived 31 months at sea:

> 'His ship was very small, went very ill, and when we took leave of him, he remained as it were at anchor. How much he must have suffered in so bad a vessel, may well be conceived'.

Carteret was painfully aware of the contrast between the two ships: the *Boudeuse* 'sailed so much better, that they went by us, as if we had been at Anchor, altho' we had a fine fresh gale, and all the sails we could sett'. The young Frenchman who came on board with the story that the *Boudeuse* had been on a trading trip to Sumatra soon raised Carteret's suspicions with his persistent and pertinent questions about their voyage. Although Carteret did not rise to the bait he was mortified to hear after the ship's parted company that one of the French sailors had bragged to the *Swallow's* quartermaster that the *Boudeuse* had also been on a voyage around the world.

Although he was surprised 'that men of Character; could be so absurd, as to endeavour to pass for what they were not', Carteret had gleaned some interesting information from the encounter. He had learnt that Wallis had discovered Tahiti, which was, according to the *Gazette de France*, 'une nouvelle Isle, grande, fertile et bien peuplee' (a new island, large, fertile and well populated) and it was to be the destination of a new Royal Navy expedition which would 'iront a la recherche de la Corvette *l'Hirondelle*, qui se separa du *Dolphin*, le 9 Avril 1767,' (they will go in search of the frigate *Swallow* which separated from the *Dolphin* on the 9th April 1767) and they will 'essayeront de decouvrir le Continent Meridional' (endeavour to discover the Southern Continent.) Even as the *Boudeuse* and *Swallow* met, Captain Cook's *Endeavour* had already rounded Cape Horn and entered the South Pacific Ocean, where his subsequent discoveries would eclipse those made by Wallis, Bougainville and Carteret.

Bougainville went on to have a long and illustrious career receiving many honours from the French Government. Carteret, however, received no recognition from the Admiralty for his achievements, his naval career stalled and it was ten years before he received another commission. The depth of his disillusion with the service he loved so much and had served so loyally can be judged by his determination 'that neither of his sons should be brought up either for the Navy or Army Professions'. Thanks to his children's unwavering belief in the importance of his circumnavigation, the records that Carteret had kept so meticulously were carefully preserved and the 'sacred relics', as his son describes them, are papers divided between the State Library of New South Wales, Australia and the National Maritime Museum, Greenwich. This account of the life of a 'neglected and gallant' officer is based on those papers, the majority of which were edited by Helen Wallis and published in two volumes by the Hakluyt Society in 1965.

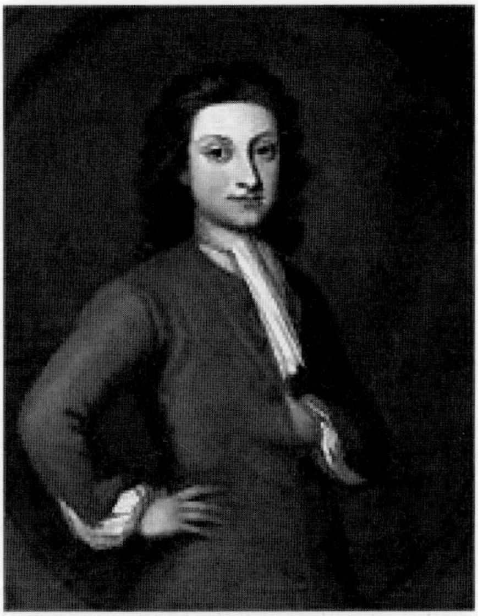

Philip De Carteret

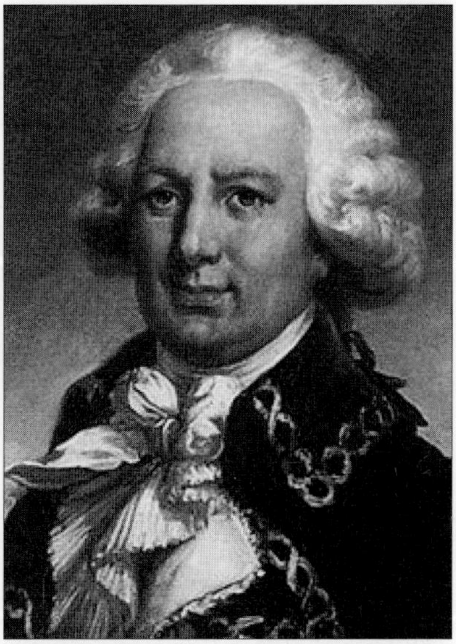

Louis-Antoine de Bougainville

Notes

The term His Majesty's Ship or HMS was not generally applied to Royal Naval vessels until the middle of the 19th century. Before this it was usual for Royal Navy vessels to be referred to simply by their name or to have the vessels rig follow the Royal appellation – His Majesty's Ship, His Majesty's Brig or His Majesty's Schooner. The first recorded use of the abbreviated form, "HMS", was HMS *Phoenix* in 1789.

Christened Philippe de Carteret, he is Philip Carteret in Royal Navy records and Philippe Carteret in Jersey legal documents.

Chapter 1

'To be Englisched'

In 1806 Philip de Carteret's son Philip (1776–1828), a Captain in the Royal Navy[1], was presented to King George III during an inspection of the Fleet in Weymouth Harbour; the King remarked to Queen Charlotte that 'this young man belongs to one of the most ancient and loyal families in my kingdom'. From the 11th century, when Onfroi and Maugier de Cartrait followed William the Conqueror to England and fought at the Battle of Hastings, the de Carteret family of St Ouen's had produced men distinguished in naval and military affairs as well as in the administration and government of the Channel Islands. In the 1630s and 1640s the staunchly Royalist de Carteret family held the reins of power in Jersey. Sir Philip de Carteret was Lieutenant Governor and Bailiff, a cousin was Attorney General, brother Solicitor-General and, when Philip died in 1643, his nephew and son-in-law George Carteret[2] took over his autocratic position. He was also one of the best known officers in the Navy, having the reputation of being 'as good if not the best seaman in England'. When the Civil War began, Parliament had offered him the post of Vice-Admiral, but King Charles I had forbidden him to accept. Realising that Jersey would not fight for the King he assembled his own fleet of ships, a position which was regularised in December 1644 when the King appointed him Vice-Admiral of Jersey with jurisdiction over 'all ships, men, whales, rigs and grampusses'[3] thus incorporating his private fleet into the Royal Navy.

When the shocking news of the execution of Charles I reached Jersey in February 1649 de Carteret ordered the Vicomte to proclaim his eldest son Prince Charles in the Market Place as 'by right and lawful succession our sole and sovereign lord'. Under the protection of de Carteret, Jersey offered a safe haven to Prince Charles during these troubled years and he made two visits, one in 1646 and another from September 1649 to February the following year. He expressed his gratitude for the support and loyalty de Carteret had showed him in a letter, a treasured possession of the present Seigneur of St Ouen, 'I can never forget the good services you have done to my father and me, and, if God bless me, you shall find I doe remember them to the advantage of you and yours'. On the restoration of the King in 1660 Charles kept his word and Sir George became Vice-Chamberlain of the Royal Household, a Privy Councillor and, from 1661-1667, Treasurer of the Navy. According to his employee Samuel Pepys, he was a 'man that do take the most pains, and gives himself the most to do business of any about the Court, without any desire of pleasure or divertissements'.

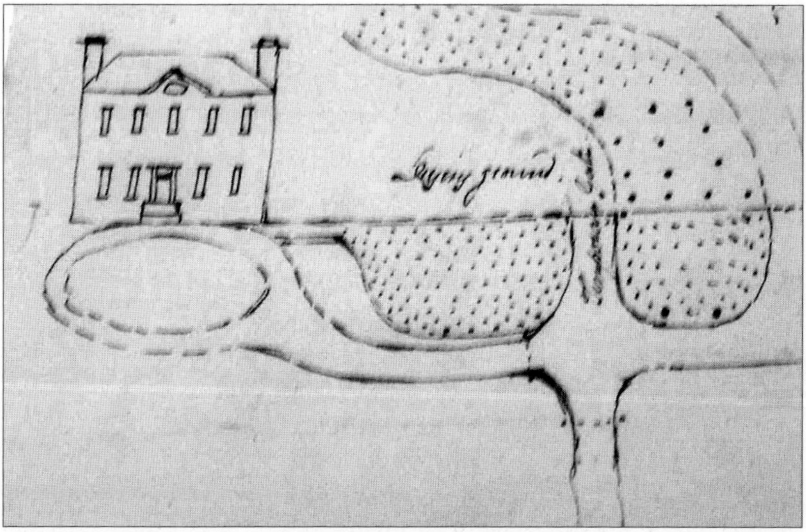

Sketch of Trinity Manor from Sir Philip Carteret Silvester's Farm Diary 1820/1.
(Societe Jersiaise Library Collection)

Like George, Philip came from the cadet branch of the de Carteret family. He was born at Trinity Manor on 22 January 1733, the third son of Charles de Carteret, the Seigneur of Trinity, and Françoise Marie St Paul. The family had acquired Trinity through the marriage in 1578 of Amias de Carteret[4] (c.1559-1631), second son of Helier de Carteret, Seigneur of St Ouen, and Catherine, the only daughter and heir of Gilles Lemprière, Seigneur of Trinity. Amias inherited the Manor in 1601 when his father-in-law died. The stone plaque impaled with the arms of his family and that of his wife remain on the façade of the house to this day. The whole Island was divided into holdings called fiefs of which the five major ones included St Ouen and Trinity. Each fief was controlled by a Seigneur who owned rights over those who lived on his land and dues had to be paid to him either in labour or in kind; these were meticulously recorded both in the *Livre des Aveux* and the sittings of the Seigneural court.

Although we know little about Philip's education prior to his entry into the Navy at the age of 14, it is likely that he followed family tradition and was a scholar at Winchester College where he would have gained fluency in English, a vital part of the process of becoming 'englisched', as a contemporary quaintly termed it. The everyday language of the Island was Jèrriais, a variation of French, but increasingly English was spoken, a process which had began with the merchant classes who were trading with England and also among those dealing with the officers and men of the English regiments sent to garrisons in Jersey.

John Bechervaise, a merchant sailor who was educated in Jersey and England in the late 18th century, did not find the experience of being *englisched* a very happy one:

> 'Of all the inhabitants of our little Island, very few then spoke English, and any youth who was happy enough to get any thing like an English education was considered as something superior to other Islanders'.

When John got to his school in Southampton he found that not one scholar spoke French:

> 'the little English I had learnt in Jersey having only been picked up here and there, I seldom used, and whenever I spoke it only raised a laugh at my expense...the boys...would plague and vex me in order to make me speak English, and then laugh at my foreign accent'. (Sir George Carteret never lost his pronounced French accent.)

Philip's early love of the sea made a career in the Royal Navy an obvious choice so, on 12 July 1747, at the age of 14, he left Jersey for Plymouth where he was to join the *Salisbury*[5] as the servant of its Captain, George Edgcumbe, the second son of Richard 1st Baron Edgcumbe of Mount Edgcumbe House. Entering the Navy as a servant was the usual method of employment for young men of good families who hoped to become commissioned officers. Becoming an officer's servant and under his patronage or that of other friends or connections helped the young sailor to gain experience and to serve the qualifying time of two years before serving as a midshipman or master's mate. However his naval career did not get off to a very auspicious start. When he arrived at Plymouth Harbour he was devastated to find that his ship had left port two days before he arrived and was not due back until October. Fortunately he found lodgings 'at one Mistress Surrow who then kept the sign of Mount Edgcumbe house, and married while I stay'd with her Lieutenant Gilliard and I went and lodged with them'.

When Philip joined the Royal Navy, Britain was still involved in the War of Austrian Succession, an eight-year conflict during which Britain sided with Austria, Holland and against France and Spain. The expansion and consolidation of British colonies and trade was dependant on the supremacy of the Royal Navy both in home waters and further afield. Smaller warships like the *Salisbury* played an essential role in this strategy. Acting independently of the main fleet they could cover a much wider area and it was during one of these patrols that the *Salisbury* captured a wealthy French East Indiaman, an event which is alluded to in Sir Joshua Reynolds's portrait of Edgcumbe painted in 1748 (see plate 2). Resplendent in full dress uniform the Captain stands in front of two columns, an indication that the setting is the family home, Mount Edgcumbe. The mansion was situated on the heights above Plymouth Sound, the guns of the battery below are clearly visible in the bottom left-hand corner and the *Salisbury* itself can be seen in the middle distance silhouetted against a stormy sky. The exotic nature of the cargo of the captured ship is represented by a wydah (an African long-tailed paradise bird) perched on some trailing ivy.

Victories by Admirals Anson and Hawke against the French fleet brought the War to a close in 1748 with Britain's ascendancy at sea well established. Philip was discharged from the *Salisbury* on 2 January 1748, his passing certificate shows that he had 15 months' service in the capacity of officer's servant. In January 1751 he joined the *Monmouth*[6] as a volunteer, spending much time ferrying soldiers from Plymouth to Gibraltar and the British Naval Base at Port Mahon on the island of Minorca, the first British overseas dockyard. On 22 November 1751 Philip transferred from the *Monmouth* to the *St Albans*[7]: it was a move which was to alter the course of his life. The commander of the ship was Captain John Byron (see plate 3). Ten years older than Carteret he had been a midshipman on the *Wager*, a store ship which had been part of Admiral Anson's squadron which had been sent into the Pacific by the British Government to attack Spanish interests along the west coast of South America and to try to find a base for the British Navy in the South Atlantic.

Anson's squadron was at sea from 1740 to 1744. The success of the circumnavigation and the capture of an exceptionally valuable Spanish prize was, however, negated by the appalling effects of 'that horrid disorder', scurvy, of nearly 2,000 men who set out in a fleet of seven ships only about 200 returned. Anson's flagship *Centurion* was the only ship which completed its mission, the rest were wrecked, scuttled or forced back to England in a shattered condition. Scurvy is caused by a cocktail of vitamin deficiencies, of which vitamin C is the most important. It can be found in fresh fruit and vegetables but is most concentrated in citrus fruit. The chemical name for vitamin C, ascorbic acid, is derived from the Latin word for scurvy, *scorbutus*, and a lack of it in the diet eventually causes a breakdown in the cellular structure of the body. Pascoe Thomas was on board the *Centurion*, when he found that black spots spread over his body:

> 'till almost my legs and thighs were as black as a negro...and this accompanied with such excessive pains in the Joints of the Knees, Ancles and Toes.... It next advanced to the Mouth; all my teeth were presently loose, and my Gums, over-charged with extravasted Blood, fell down almost quite over my Teeth'.

These extreme physical symptoms were accompanied by intense depression, lethargy and homesickness, a state, which was called 'scorbutic nostalgia'.

Guernseyman Philip Saumarez joined the fleet as a third lieutenant; by the end of the voyage he had been promoted to Captain and was Anson's second-in-command (he was the uncle of Admiral James Saumarez, one of Nelson's 'band of brothers'). In the 1960s his four original logbooks were discovered in a battered cardboard box at the back of a cupboard in the family's home Sausmarez Manor. They tell a tragic story. In April 1741 the squadron encountered terrible storms whilst rounding the Cape Horn. On 23 April when Anson ordered him to go on board the *Centurion* (original complement 399 men and 122 marines) he found that almost everyone was infected with the scurvy and badly demoralised. On each watch no more than 70 seamen could be mustered, while all the marines were either sick or dead. When they took

> 'the tarpaulins off the gratings and hatchways to air between decks and clean the ship as much as lay in our power; and really it is scarce conceivable what a stench and nastyness our poor sick people had caused among each other and which contributed to infect those who struggled against distemper....Our men now began to decline a pace, the scurvy reigning among us and making terrible havoc'.

Byron was away from England for even longer, en route to the squadron's rendezvous at the island of Juan Fernandez. The *Wager* had become separated and was being driven towards the Gulf of Penas on the Patagonian coast, an area which the Captain's charts did not cover in any detail. In mountainous seas and with a full gale blowing out of the west, every sail was torn and the rigging unsecured. The *Wager* struck a submerged rock at 4.30 a.m., drifted off badly holed and then became lodged between two giant boulders. When dawn broke the 140 survivors who scrambled ashore found they were on a desolate island off the south coast of Chile in the middle of the harsh Patagonian winter. The few who remained on board became roaring drunk and Captain Cheap was incapable of dealing with a situation in which the survivors split into two opposing factions. Byron and the officers supported Captain Cheap whilst the other group, which included a number of soldiers not under naval discipline, found its leader in the gunner John Bulkeley, 'a warrant officer of formidable personality'.

Bulkeley took the *Wager*'s longboat *Speedwell* and 59 men south from the wreck through the straits of Magellan and up the east coast of South America while the Captain took 19 men and went north up the coast to the Spanish colonial capital Santiago. Unbelievably both parties, their numbers drastically reduced, eventually reached England after adventures and deprivations which tested the limits of human endurance. Five of the survivors published accounts of their ordeals. Byron's description of the shipwreck in his *Account of the Great Distresses suffered by himself and his Companions* inspired his grandson Lord Bryon when he was writing his poetic masterpiece *Don Juan* and the drama of the tragedy also left its mark on his narrative poem *Childe Harold*. In 2006 the Scientific Exploration Society under the leadership of Colonel Blashford-Snell located four metres of a wooden hull in the waters where the *Wager* foundered, the date of the wood was shown by carbon dating to be the correct date for the *Wager*.

The Royal Navy's role in securing 'The advancement of the Trade and Navigation of Great Britain' was the reason behind Byron's mission in 1751, when the *St Albans, Sphinx, Assurance* and *Badger* were sent to the coast of Guinea on the western coast of Africa. France and England battled throughout the first half of the 18th century for control of the Guinea coast; slaves from that area supplied the labour for the immensely valuable sugar plantations in the West Indies. The Royal Navy was sent to patrol the area in case the French attempted to claim the coastline for themselves. Carteret's *Memorandum of Service* shows that three French warships were challenged when it was discovered they had forced the locals to build a fort. On 21 February 1752 they anchored off Amassa where a deal was made with the local inhabitants to take the ships' empty water casks and fill them up, a necessary arrangement as the surf 'brake so high on the beach that none of our boats are able to land for which trouble we paid them with a little rum and tobacco'. The ships then proceeded along the coastline where 'several of the Brittinick forts saluted us'. When they reached the island of St Thomas in St Charlotte Bay owned by the Portuguese, the ships went their separate ways and on 10 April 1752 they sailed for England.

Carteret now followed Byron from ship to ship. Discharged from the *St Albans* in October he spent the Christmas in Jersey, then joined two ships under the command of Byron, the *Augusta*[8] and the *Vanguard*[9]. According to his certificate of discharge from the *Vanguard* he had attained the rank of Midshipman. The document signed by Byron on 22 October 1753 and was witnessed by Rick Truelan (master), Shephard (purser) and John Penlouvich (boatswain). The amount of the Ticket was assessed at £12.4s.0d to be paid, a note in Carteret's hand shows, to Mr Francis Delacombe, a clerk in the Navy Board.

From October 1753 until April 1757, Carteret again served in the *Vanguard*, sailing mainly in Mediterranean waters, a posting which was interrupted in August 1755 when he 'Got liberty to go to London for to Pass my Examination for a Lieutenant'. The examination held on the first Wednesday of every month at the Admiralty building in Whitehall was conducted by three captains. The candidate was required to produce his journals and certificates of service and would then sit an oral exam designed to assess his knowledge of seamanship, navigation and practical skills like splicing rope and reefing sails. However passing the exam did not automatically mean that a commission was forthcoming and a successful applicant could wait years for a ship. The most telling indication of an officer's professional fortunes were his age on reaching the rank of Post-Captain and the time which elapsed from his first commission as Lieutenant. Philip gained the rank of First Lieutenant and an independent command in June 1764 aged 31 years, this was a relatively old age to achieve such rank in the Navy and was probably due to the fact that he had not served in one of the main theatres of naval activity where his ability would commend him to the leading British officers. It would be these senior naval officers who would later be in a position of influence on the Board of Admiralty. The extent to which his naval career stalled can be judged from the fact that he then had to wait another seven years before he was promoted to Post-Captain.

On 22 May 1756 Carteret was on board the *Vanguard* when 'His Majestys Declaration of War against the French King Vassals and Subjects' was read out to the assembled company. It was the beginning of the Seven Years War and it ended, for the time being, Carteret's close association with Byron as the two men went on to serve in different areas of action. Byron was in the Channel fleet and the North American station whereas Carteret joined the *Dunkirk*[10], a 60 gun fourth-rate ship which was part of a squadron of small ships guarding the Channel Islands. The commander of the fleet was Captain Howe who went on to be Lord Howe, Vice-Admiral of England, First Lord of the Admiralty and victor of the memorable Battle of 1 June in 1794. During the course of Howe's posting he met Jerseyman Charles d'Auvergne, the aide-de-camp of the 3rd Duke of Marlborough; it was the beginning of a close friendship between the two men. When Charles' son Philip joined the Royal Navy in 1770 Howe's patronage enabled him to swiftly progress through the ranks (in contrast to Carteret he gained his first independent command at the age of 23).

The year 1759 was a remarkable one in English history called the *Annus Mirabilis*, the 'Year of Victories'. A succession of naval and military successes enabled the country to eclipse France as a global power, the Royal Navy gained almost total supremacy of the seas and the foundations were laid for the creation of the first British Empire. In North America General Wolfe's victory over the French at Quebec was a momentous one as it meant that New France came under the control of England, ultimately leading to the creation of Canada. An allied Anglo-German army defeated the French at the Battle of Minden. Guadeloupe was captured from the French in the West Indies and in India a French attack on Madras in India was repulsed. From 1757 to 1762 Carteret served on the *Guernsey*[11], a 50 gun fourth rate ship based mainly in the Mediterranean. By 1759 he had attained the rank of Second Lieutenant. The *Guernsey* joined Admiral Boscawen's fleet of 14 ships-of-the-line and on 18 August the squadron achieved a stunning victory over the French at Lagos (off the coast of Portugal) driving ashore and destroying *Ocean*, the 80 gun flagship and *Redoubtable*, 74 guns, and capturing the *Temeraire*, 74 guns, (the subject of Turner's famous painting of 1839) and the *Modeste*, 64 guns.

The year after his gruelling voyage Admiral Lord Anson joined the Admiralty Board and was First Lord from 1751 until his death in 1761. During that time the efficiency of his administration and the strategic reforms he introduced laid the ground for the great sea victories of the Seven Years War and the consequent expansion of the British Empire. The reforms he introduced covered all aspects of naval life from the inspection and overhauling of the dockyards, improvement of naval signal tactics, the introduction of copper bottoming, a standard uniform for naval officers, a new class of 36-gun frigate and improved victualling of the navy and the sanitary arrangements on board. His greatest contribution, however, was the selection and promotion of a series of naval officers of genius who enabled the Navy to attain an unprecedented pitch of power and pre-eminence. The French writer Voltaire observed that:

> 'As trade enriched the citizens in England so it combined to their freedom, and this freedom on the other side extended their commerce, whence arose the grandeur of the state. Trade raised by insensible degrees the naval power, which gives the English superiority over the seas, and they are now masters of very near 200 ships of war'.

The need to protect these trading interests was a prime motive behind the next voyage that Carteret embarked on but before that, he had a pressing personal matter to attend to. In September 1761 his older brother Francis had died and Philip inherited a property so encumbered with debt that he practically had to buy it back (the accounts show that in 1752 their mother Françoise had taken out two sizeable loans to be paid back over a 12-year period, two further loans followed in 1757 and 1761). A note in Philip's hand on an inventory of the *Meuble du Manoir a la Mort de mon grand grand-pere* shows that in 1696 the contents of the manor were in a very sorry state. It stated that since the Civil War no repairs to furniture had been made and when Charles de Carteret, his great-grandfather died, he left everything so poor, so shabby and so much in rags (*si pauvre, si use et si en guenilles*) that the family were so embarrassed they did not want people to visit. Mattresses and feather beds had all been repaired but the latter were so thin and empty they were no longer of any use. There were five sets of bed hangings of which three were in rags and two had been ruined by rats. It would appear from a court action lodged in 1740 that Philip's father, who had died in 1737, had been living on credit, the demands of dozens of creditors were listed against 'the estate of the said Lordship as the ignoble estate and the moveable and chatteled estate of the said deceased seized and possessed were subject to the payment of debt'.

In 1641-2 Amice de Carteret had extended the house by adding two bays to the west. This had the effect of placing the original entrance to the house off centre, the unusually large front door (48" wide and 8' 2" high), elevated by a couple of stone steps is flanked on one side by four windows and two on the right. Further alterations to the façade of the house were made around 1700 when Philip's grandfather Charles (1646-1712) added fashionable sash windows with thick glazing bars. Two sketches of the house were made around 1820, one by Philip's son and the other by Fanny Le Maistre, daughter of the Constable of Trinity. In Fanny's sketch there is a substantial dwelling house to the right of the building which was probably part of the farm complex. Family documents show that the Manor was self-sufficient in producing its own dairy products, fruit and vegetables and there were horses, oxen, cows, sheep and other livestock. The tree in the foreground is today of such enormous girth and height it lends credence to the story that the future Charles II sat underneath it whilst visiting the Seigneur in 1646. In fact it has been identified as a Lucombe oak *Querus cerris (Lucombeana)*, so called because the variety was first raised in a nursery in Exeter in 1762 by a Mr Lucombe.

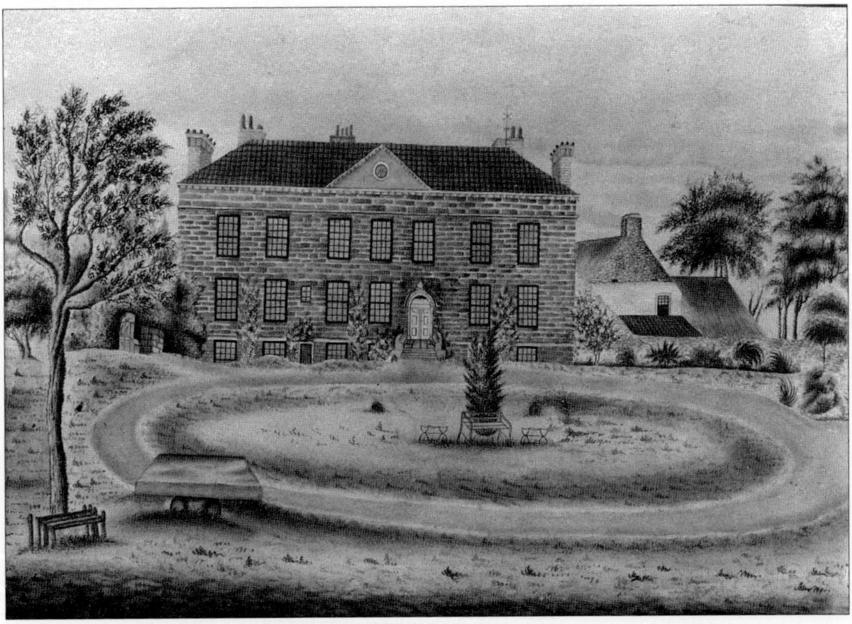

Sketch of Trinity Manor by Fanny Le Maistre around 1820,
(Société Jersiaise Library Collection)

Anne, Philip's sister, was entrusted with running the Manor and on 4 March 1764 she received a letter from Byron, asking her where he could find her brother. On the 12 March he wrote to Carteret himself:

> 'If you should Chuse to go to Sea with me, make all the Haste you can to Town as not a Moment's time must be lost'.

Chapter 2

'The Key to the Pacific Ocean'

Byron had a very successful war; from 1757 until early 1760 he cruised off the coast of France in Admiral Sir Edward Hawke's fleet or in command of his own squadron. His ship was the *America*[1] and then in 1759 he was given command of the newly commissioned the *Fame*[2], 74 guns. In 1760 he was ordered to cross the Atlantic where, following the demolition of the fort at Louisberg, Cape Breton, he lead a squadron of two other ships-of-the-line[3] and two frigates *Scarborough* (29) and *Repulse* (32) in the destruction of a French convoy of 20 schooners and sloops along with the 28-gun frigate *Machault* and two armed merchant ships: the *Marquis de Malauze* (16 guns), and the *Bienfaisant* (12 guns) carrying troops and stores intended for the relief of Quebec[4]. Byron remained in Canada for the rest of the year before he returned to England and he spent the rest of the war serving on the blockade of Brest.

When the War ended the Admiralty had again turned its attention to a voyage of exploration to the South Pacific as it was considered essential for Britain to have a base in the far south for further exploration and to open up new areas for trade and enterprise. Lord Egmont was First Lord of the Admiralty from 1763 to 1766 and, acting under conditions of the greatest secrecy, he instructed Byron to survey and take possession of the Falkland Islands. He was to pass through the Strait of Magellan, proceed up the Pacific coast of South and North America and search for a passage back to the North Atlantic through Hudson's Bay. He was also 'to make enquiries after the People who were shipwrecked in His Majesty's ship the *Wager*[5] and left upon that Coast, and use your best endevours to bring them home with you'. The political sensitivity of the mission was such that a subterfuge had to be found in case the French and Spanish heard about the real aim of the voyage. Byron's official commission was Commander-in-Chief of an expedition to the East Indies. The surgeon, believing they were heading for the 'sickly climate' of the Indian waters, spent more than £90 of his own money on special supplies.

The Falkland Islands had been discovered in 1592 by Captain John Davis and in the following year Hawkins had taken formal possession of them in the name of Queen Elizabeth I but, until Anson's voyage of 1740-4, they had been ignored. Anson, however, could see their potential as a base and the advantages of this project had been set out in Walter's edition of his voyage which was published in 1748. The Admiralty had taken up the project in 1749 and was preparing an expedition when Spanish protests led the Government to abandon the scheme. The project appeared in an entirely different light after Britain's successes against Spain in the closing months of the Seven Years War, but possession of the Islands was not only a contentious issue between Britain and Spain, the French circumnavigator Louis Antoine de Bougainville (1729-1811) had already claimed them for France nearly a year before. Antoine Joseph Pernetty, a Benedictine monk, sailed with Bougainville on the *Aigle*[6] and published an account of the journey in 1771:

> 'We had taken possession of these islands in the beginning of April 1764, before the *Dolphin* was off the stocks, and we quitted them the 8th of the same month on our return to France, where we landed the 26th June. The English did not sail till some days after'.

The English did indeed sail a few days later. Byron left Plymouth on 3 July 1764 in the *Dolphin*[7] (24 guns, 150 men), Carteret joining him as First Lieutenant on the frigate *Tamar*[8] (14 guns, 90 men). They put in at the Cape Verde islands for fresh water and reached Rio de Janeiro on 12 September, sailing from there on 21 October. The ships passed down the coast of Patagonia following the track on the chart published in Anson's Voyage and consequently the one followed by the *Wager* when Byron was serving as a midshipman 20 years earlier. From 21 November until 5 December they were anchored at Port Desire at the mouth of the Deseado River in the Santa Cruz province of Argentina but were unable to find fresh water and firewood there. However, they did find 'the barrel of a musket, with the King's broad arrow upon it, the musket barrel had suffered so much from the weather, that it might be crumbled into dust between the fingers'. Another possible clue to the plight of the survivors of the *Wager* occurred when an Indian family approached one of Byron's officers and seemed to be offering a girl who 'had tolerable features, and an English face'.

On 21 December they approached the eastern entrance to the Strait of Magellan and arrived at the place where Bulkeley in the *Wager's* longboat *Speedwell* had seen a number of horsemen inviting them to come ashore. When Byron looked through his telescope he also saw 'a number of horsemen riding backward and forward directly a-breast of the ship, and waving something white, as a invitation to come on shore'. Byron decided to investigate, he set off in the *Dolphin's* twelve-oared boat with a 'party of men, very well armed'. The First Lieutenant, with a separate party, followed in another. As they approached the shoreline they could see that some 500 people, accompanied by innumerable yelping dogs, had gathered together on a stony point of land. Byron advanced alone. When the Indians fell back, he made a sign that one of them should come forward. Their chief, 'a frightful colossus' over six feet tall, had a circle of black paint round one eye and a white circle round the other, the rest of his face was painted in streaks of various colours. He had the skin of an animal, with the hair inwards slung over his shoulder 'like a tartan plaid'. This Indian tribe had first been seen by Magellan who called them *Patagones*, the Spanish word for big feet. In 1586 the English explorer Sir Thomas Cavendish had measured the imprint of one of their feet and found it to be 18 inches long, his account and that of other early explorers had fixed the race in the public imagination as being giants and consequently the country had come to be known as Patagonia.

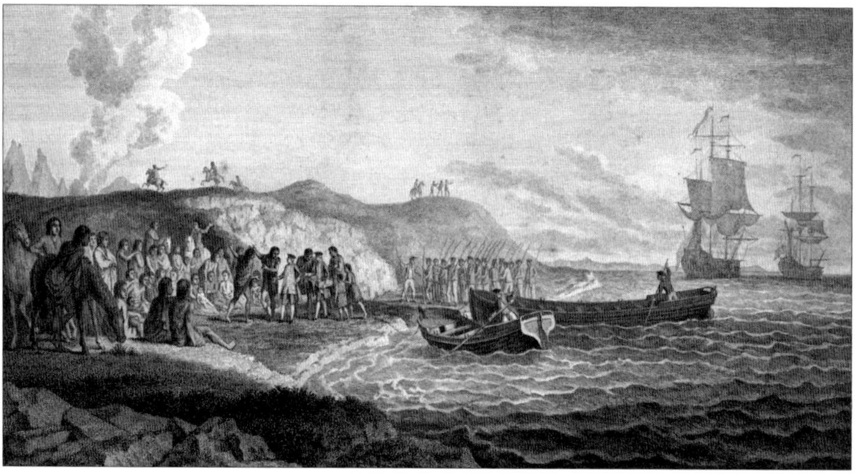

The meeting between Byron and the Patagonians in December 1764 from Hawkesworth's An account of the voyages...Southern Atmosphere, *1773*

Conversing entirely in sign language, Byron handed out yellow and white beads, tobacco and lengths of green silk ribbon, gifts that were received with much appreciation and enjoyment but he declined an offer to go inland with the chief and see their settlement. Although eyewitness accounts agreed that the average height of these people was about six feet on their return to England some of the junior officers could not resist adding many more inches to their height, Midshipman Charles Clarke, for example, told the Royal Society that 'there was hardly a man there less than 8 feet, most of them considerably more'. These sensational accounts created, according to Carteret, 'much noise in Europe and particularly in England', a reaction that was probably encouraged by the British Government for it had the effect of diverting attention from the real reason for Byron's voyage.

Still looking for supplies of firewood they continued to sail up the Strait of Magellan until 26 December when they anchored at Port Famine[9] and found a huge amount of drift-wood on the beach. Food supplies were also improved by a plentiful supply of fish and a number of geese and duck were shot by Byron.

On 7 January 1765 they sailed for the Falkland Islands. When they were sighted on the 12th, Byron took bearings and soundings and sent the boats in to look for a harbour. When they found a splendid one on the 15th Byron took possession of the island in the name of the King and called the harbour Port Egmont after the First Lord of the Admiralty[10]. They found that 'fresh water in the greatest plenty, and geese, ducks, snipes and other birds are so numerous that our people grew tired of them'. There was also an abundance of seafood: mussels, clams, cockles and limpets enlivened the ship's diet along with wild celery and wood sorrel. Byron then returned to the South American mainland to Port Desire[11] where he met the store ship *Florida*[12] which he brought to the Strait of Magellan in order to find shelter from the incessant gales and transfer her cargo to the *Dolphin* and the *Tamar*. Vital repairs to the *Florida's* mast and the *Tamar's* rudder were effected by the forge, which they had brought with them; they transferred it to the shore and secured the rudder with iron clamps. It was at this point that *Florida* encountered a French ship with 'a great number of officers on board'. Byron later learnt that this was Bougainville's *Eagle* supplying the settlement he had established on the Falkland Islands at Port Louis[13] with firewood.

The *Dolphin* and *Tamar* carried on through the Strait, the scenery of 'craggy mountains...on each side, towering above the clouds, and covered with everlasting snow (had) the most dreary and desolate apperance that can be imagined'. It rained incessantly, 'every man on board being on deck the whole time, and everyone wet to the skin, for the rain, or rather sheets of water...did not cease a moment'. Byron was worried that the combined effect of the cold and lack of dry clothing would have a bad effect on the health and morale of the crews and so he decided to distribute two bales of a stout, thick woollen fabric called fearnought to all the officers and men. Cut and sewn to a rudimentary pattern it made a 'comfortable and salutary jacket'. Formerly used for covering portholes and the doors of powder magazines this was the first time it had been used as a protective garment and the fearnought jacket or Magellan jacket, as it was sometimes described, became a standard item of uniform in the Royal Navy.

It took two months to get through the Strait to the Pacific Ocean. The fierce westerly gales were relentless and on 28 March the two ships were anchored in a little bay opposite Cape Quod[14] (see plate 5) when the cables to the *Tamar's* bower-anchor[15] parted and the ship narrowly escaped being dashed to pieces against the rocks. The *Dolphin* went to her assistance after which they anchored for the night only to experience the most dreadful storm anyone on board had experienced. The winds 'were so violent they tore up the sea and carried it higher then the tops of the masts, a dreadful sea rolled over them and broke against the rocks with a noise as loud as thunder'. Fortunately their cables did not part and they did not suffer the fate of the *Wager*.

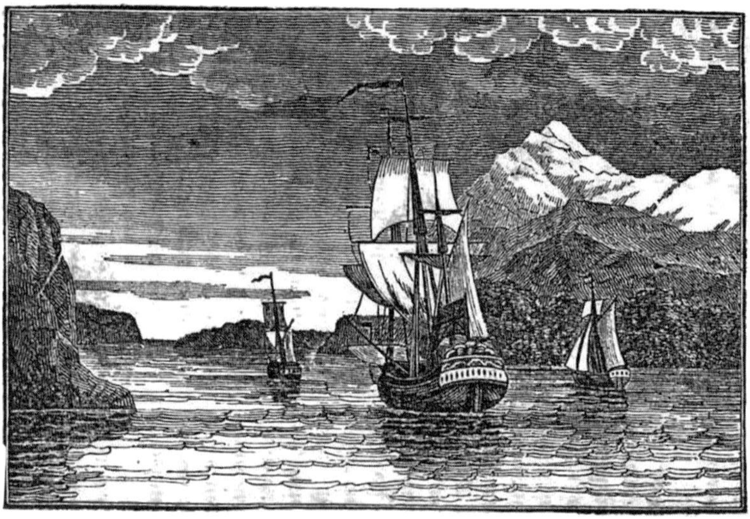

The Straits of Magellan

On 9 April they finally reached the Pacific Ocean. Byron sailed northwards following the coast of Chile until, on 28 April, they anchored at Masa Fuero, the most western island in the Juan Fernandez group. Now that they were in the Pacific Ocean, Byron took the title of Commodore and reorganised his officers. Carteret's navigational skills made him more useful to Byron on the *Dolphin* and so he was transferred to that ship with the rank of First Lieutenant, a fortuitous move for had he remained on the *Tamar* he would not have reached England until 23 July 1766 and would have been out of the running for inclusion in the second circumnavigation.

Two days later they left the relative security of Masa Fuero for the vast, uncharted waters of the Pacific hoping they would find a 'Place of Consquence in the South Seas'. A key landfall in that exploration were the legendary Solomon Islands; they had been discovered by the Spanish explorer Alvaro de Mendana in 1568 and as he claimed that the Islands were the source of King Solomon's legendary gold, all of Europe had been keen to rediscover them. It was also believed that the Islands were the outposts of Terra Australis Incognita, the great southern continent. Mendana and his Portuguese pilot, Pedro Fernandez de Quiros, led another expedition to the Islands in 1595 and attempted to found a settlement on the largest island, which they called Santa Cruz. It was unsuccessful and when Quiros tried to find the Islands again in 1605 he could not locate them.

Byron did not sight land until 7 June when they saw the islands of Tepoto. The Island had the 'most beautiful apperance' and the sailors could see the coconuts and vegetation but 'the great surf all round it' made it impossible to land. The intense frustration endured by all on board at being unable to land in the 'little Paradise which Nature had forbidden them to enter'; led Byron to call them the 'Islands of Disappointment'.

After two months at sea it was now essential to find fresh fruit and vegetables as scurvy was beginning to affect the crews of both ships and on 10 June they landed on Takakoroa and Takapoto Islands which Byron called King George's Islands. Now known as the Tuamotu Archipelago this complex of 76 small islands and atolls was the expedition's closest landfall to Tauiti and the whole archipelago of the Society Islands. Despite the 'intolerable torment of flies which covered us from head to foot' they filled their longboats with 'loads of coconuts and a great quantity of scurvy-grass'[16]. Until this point the natives they had seen had been on shore 'armed with clubs and spears, using threatening gestures' but on 2 July the ship was approached by 60 canoes or proas as they were known. They formed a circle round the ship and eventually one of the most adventurous natives swam over to the ship and nimbly climbed up the side, he then promptly sat down on the gunwale. He then

> 'burst into a violent fit of laughter, started up, and ran all over the ship, attempting to steal whatever he could lay his hands upon, but without success, for being stark naked, it was impossible to conceal his booty for a

> moment. Our seamen put him on a jacket and trowsers, which produced great merriment...after having played a thousand antic tricks, he leapt overboard, jacket and trowsers and all, and swam back to his proa'.

Byron now had his last opportunity to fulfill his mission, although the Pacific was studded with innumerable unknown archipelagos which, if the two ships had split up and followed a zigzagging course, could have been explored. At the crucial moment he altered course a great swell had come up from the south and he was afraid that the ships could be rolled over. He went on to discover a few not very important islands but became increasingly preoccupied with the sickness of the crews in both ships for they were creating 'an inescapable impediment'. By 21 July when all the coconuts had been consumed 'our people began to fall down again with the Scurvy...some of my best men already so bad in it, that they are confined to their Hammocks'. It was vital to land and get more coconuts for Byron believed that the beneficial effect of the fruit was found to be

> 'astonishing; many whose limbs were become as black as ink, who could not move without the assistance of two men, and who, besides total debility, suffered excruciating pain, were in a few days, by eating these nuts, although at sea, so far recovered as to do their duty'.

He sailed in a northerly direction to the Mariana Islands landing at Tinian and from 31 July until 30 September, they stayed on the island using the forge to repair the ironwork. There was, however, no respite from the intense, suffocating heat and being 'incessantly tormented by the flies in the day and by mosquitoes in the night'.

Leaving Tinian they sailed down the west side of the Philippines through the Spratly Islands and on 30 October anchored off Pulo Timoan off the east coast of Malaya. It was obvious to Byron that he had been right to call a halt to exploration when he did:

> 'We now had nothing to eat but the ship's provisions, which were become very bad, for all our beef and pork stunk intolerably, and our bread was rotten and full of worms'.

Although his crew recovered and he could have gone north to search for the North West Passage he chose to return to England. He reached Batavia in the Dutch East Indies[17] on 28 November, rounded the Cape of Good Hope in February 1766 and finally sighted the Isles of Scilly on 7 May 1766.

No doubt Carteret, who had a reputation for being adventurous, impatient and somewhat intolerant was intensely frustrated by Byron's decision to return home without further exploration, but Byron's decision to investigate the eastern and central Pacific, for which there was no mandate in his official instructions, meant that on his return Egmont decided on a radical change of objective and the search for the southern continent was officially transferred to this region. Byron may not have been a dedicated explorer but his horrendous experiences following the shipwreck of the *Wager* must have shaped his attitudes and it was his constant solicitude for his men that made him turn back when he might have gone on. His greatest success was to prove that the Anson's disastrous voyage, when more than half the crew died from scurvy, could be prevented. Only six men died in the *Dolphin* and the *Tamar* during the two years they were at sea.

When the ships finally anchored, the official reaction to their exploration of the Pacific was somewhat mixed. On the one hand the Royal Society severely criticised the expedition for 'a dearth of scientific results' (Byron commented somewhat acidly that the discovery of any more islands would have been at the cost of his sailors' lives). Lord Egmont, on the other hand, was delighted Byron had succeeded in acquiring a key objective – the Falkland Islands – and his subsequent observations confirmed Egmont's belief that a 'southern continent' lay to the south of King George's Islands in the Tuamutu Archipelago.

Egmont believed there was no time to waste if Britain's position was to be consolidated and a second expedition had to be dispatched immediately. Circumstantial evidence suggests that Byron took a leading part in planning the voyage and it would have been on his personal recommendation that Carteret had a prominent role in it.

The timetable for organising the expedition was, however, affected by an unexpected twist in international politics, a development that was destined to have near disastrous consequences for Carteret. On 19 May 1766 the Spanish had persuaded the French Government to hand over their settlement in the Falklands, Les Isles Malouines, in return for compensation to its founder Bougainville. Effectively the Islands would then be possessed by the Spaniards who, from their South American base, would make short work of any colony entirely dependant on Europe for supplies and men and Britain's tenuous foothold from which to explore the Pacific would be placed in jeopardy. Even more worryingly Egmont also discovered that the French were hoping to find and lay claim to 'Les Terres Australes'. It was vital to win government and royal consent for the immediate dispatch of the expedition.

The Cabinet met on 3 June in the office of Lieutenant General Henry Seymour-Conway[18], Secretary of State for the Northern Department, and approved Egmont's *Expedition to Falkland Islands and discoveries in the Southern part of the World.* However, Egmont was opposed in the Cabinet by a rival group within government, headed by the Duke of Grafton, who were determined to stop the expedition from sailing for they feared that it would precipitate a final rupture with France and Spain. On 1 July it was

> 'resolved that Philip Carteret, late of the *Dolphin* be appointed Commander of the *Swallow*...and that she be fitted for foreign service and Victualled to Six Months of all Species of Provisions...you are hereby required & directed to cause the utmost dispatch in getting her ready for the sea'.

The leader of the expedition was to be Captain Wallis[19] (see Plate 4) and he was assigned to the *Dolphin*.

Chapter 3

'Poor dull *Swallow*'

Carteret had been back in England for less than two months when he received an order on 5 July 1766 to take command of the *Swallow*[1] and proceed to Chatham Dockyard to get her ready 'with the utmost dispatch'. When he reached the dry dock at Chatham he was bitterly disappointed. Having to find a ship in a hurry the Admiralty had chosen the *Swallow*, a sixth rate sloop of 14 guns which had been launched at Rotherhithe in 1745. It was six years older than the *Dolphin* but her 20 years of service had not been well spent. The ship had remained in the River Medway ferrying press-ganged men downriver to waiting ships. It was then assessed for repair in 1763 and, in February 1766, the repairs were made at a cost of £1,450.11s.6d, but the bottom had only been slightly sheathed with wood as a protection against worm.

Carteret later wrote that she was 'an old Vessel...and one of the worst, if not the very worst of her kind; in his Majesty's navy'. Although bulkheads had been fitted to the forepart of the quarterdeck and forecastle and the masts had been shortened to help the 'safety of the Sloop in great seas' when Carteret joined the ship on 7 July he was appalled at her obvious defects for foreign service. The next day he sent an urgent letter to Philip Stephens, Secretary of the Admiralty, asking for vital stores to be delivered. He knew from first-hand experience how important these items were; the lack of them could turn a mishap into a disaster. They included a forge that could be dismantled and reassembled when required, a small skiff which could measure the speed of currents, 'a mooring swivel in case of wintering in a Cold Country where ice is, for to preserve the cables and a sett of blocks'. He was also anxious to know which officers were going to sail with him as 'no officers of any kind, as yet have come to the Ship (except the three standing Warrant Officers)'.

In the same letter his request that the capstan be moved to the quarterdeck led to a sharp argument with the Navy Board who said 'we find the Quarter Deck is not long enough to work it upon'. His request for an awning to be

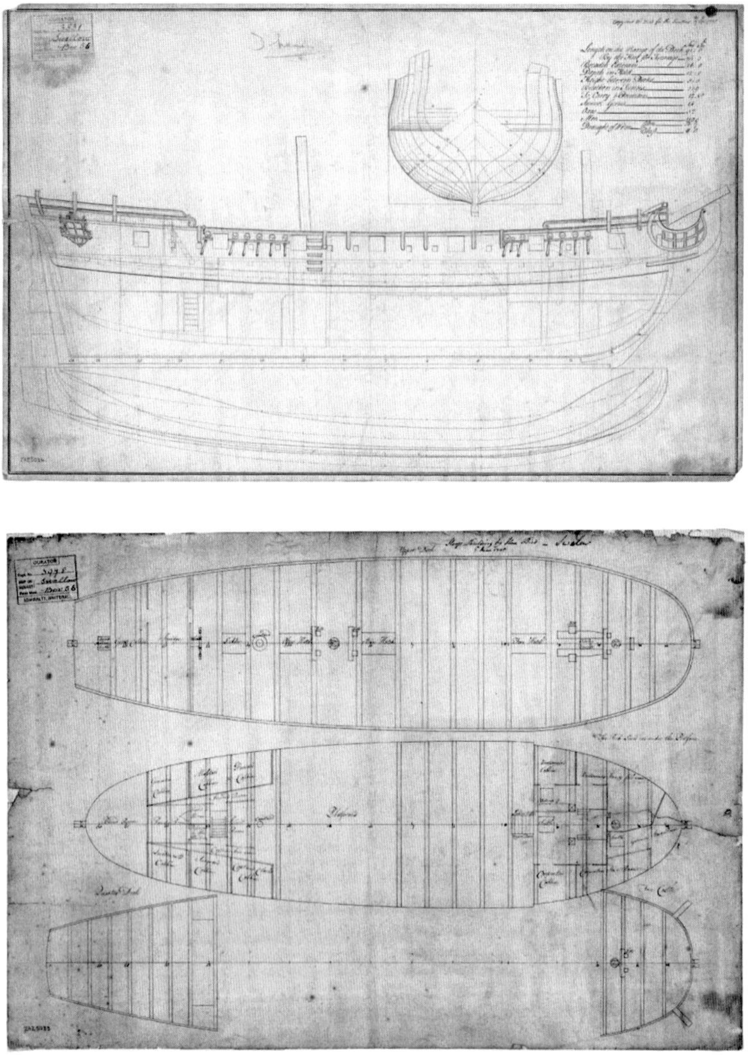

Plans of the Swallow (© *National Maritime Museum, Greenwich, London*)

constructed to that deck was also turned down. The list of stores was 'all refused me, by one of the, then Lords of the Admiralty'; his identity is revealed in Carteret's notes as Vice-Admiral Sir Charles Saunders, Second Lord of the Admiralty. The slightly sheathed bottom of the ship could not have much done to it, but when he asked for the ship to be taken into dock to be cleaned (she had been anchored in the river for over a month) this request was also refused. When Stephens later asserted that the *Swallow* was a suitable vessel properly fitted out 'for what she was intended' it is not surprising that Carteret concluded that *Swallow, Dolphin* and store ship *Prince Frederick*[2] were going to provision the settlement at Port Egmont on the Falkland Islands.

The use of copper-sheathing of ships to protect against marine growth and worms was still experimental and the *Dolphin* was only the third ship in the Royal Navy to receive it. Its advantages were not lost on Byron who wrote in 1765 that 'Copper Bottoms is the finest Invention in the world'. Although Carteret would not have expected the *Swallow* to have been sheathed, his criticism of the choice of ship was entirely justified. *Swallow* might have been a twenty year-old sloop designed to carry guns and dependable in rough water, however, it was a 'miserable tool' to take on the rigours of a voyage of exploration in which speed and manoeuvrability were the main requirements. The slowness of the *Swallow* and the heaviness of handling were all too evident when compared with the frigate *Dolphin*, which easily outstripped it – when the two ships were carrying sail the *Dolphin* covered three feet to every two covered by the *Swallow*.

These hurried preparations and the increasingly acrimonious exchange of letters between Carteret and the Admiralty had a bad effect on the recruitment of men and officers.

On 12 July, 23-year old Lieutenant Erasmus Gower joined the *Swallow* followed by the Master, Alexander Simpson, on the 18th (Simpson, Gower and the surgeon Thomas Watson had sailed on the previous voyage with Byron) and Purser Edward Leigh on the 29th. This meant that Carteret had to manage without the help of key members of the crew whilst fitting out the ship, a situation which was not made any easier on 22 July when he received a 'most pressing letter...to make all possible dispatch, in getting the *Swallow* ready for sea'. Carteret found it particularly difficult to recruit competent sailors and officers, encountering

> 'many difficulties ... in procuring men, and particularly petty officers, their pay in a Sloop, being so inadaquate to their Station, that no man of capacity will serve in them'.

Moreover this second voyage did not have the privileges, which were accorded to Byron. Wallis was not a Commodore, a flag officer who could have had a Captain serving under him. Although Carteret was called Commander or Captain because he was in command of the vessel he was still a Lieutenant. In addition to himself, the *Swallow*'s final complement of officers was a lieutenant, a master, a master's mate, two midshipmen, and five warrant officers – carpenter, gunner, boatswain, a purser and a surgeon. The small number of officers made no allowance for illness and although the Muster Book shows a complement of 108, 18 men deserted or failed to appear before sailing, 14 boys and servants were discharged so he finally sailed with 76 men plus a corporal and ten marines from the Portsmouth Division.

Samuel Wallis, Commander of the *Dolphin,* was five years older than Carteret. In 1755 he had served in the North American station as Admiral Boscawen's Flag Lieutenant and was promoted to the *Prince of Orange*[3], a 60-gun warship. In 1759 he had taken part in the siege of Quebec serving under Vice-Admiral Sir Charles Saunders, the new Commander-in-Chief of the St Lawrence Fleet. After the surrender of Quebec he joined the Channel Fleet and remained with it until the end of the War. He had the advantage of having served in one of the main theatres of naval activity under the command of Saunders, who was then given the influential position of Second Lord of the Admiralty. The decision to appoint Wallis was taken on 19 June and he received all the supplies he requested and great care was taken over the ship's repairs.

George Robertson was appointed as the *Dolphin's* Master. His detailed *Journal* about the voyage, published in 1948 by the *Hakluyt Society,* affords a fascinating and unbiased commentary on what was going on behind the scenes during the preparations for the voyage and the problems that led up to the decisive moment when the two ships parted company. It was unusual at this time for a Master (similar to the rank of Chief Petty Officer today) to keep a journal. A Master usually came from a different social class than the officers, starting as a lowly seaman he would have been promoted because he displayed a particular talent and ability. Robertson was respected for the discreet guidance he gave to 'young gentlemen officers', whilst at the same time maintaining a suitably deferential air with senior officers. He was also extremely well informed thanks to a contact at the Admiralty who made every effort to keep his friend abreast of any development that would affect the expedition. On 24 June, before Carteret received his commission, Robertson wrote:

> 'Am informed that Captain Wallis will be appointed Commodore and to hoist a Broad pendant. It is said we are all to have the same Incoragement that the Officers and men had last voyage round the world'.

When his informant revealed the real objective of the voyage and the fact that Wallis would not have the rank of Commodore, Robertson was bitterly disappointed. Not only did this mean that the crew would not receive the higher pay and other advantages which Byron's men had enjoyed, they were also embarking on a highly risky mission. Robertson wrote on 6 August:

> 'I was Informed that there is no Broad pendant to be hoisted on board the *Dolphin* and am told our Incoragement will Intirely Depend on our success in discovering a Place of Consequence in the South Sea this is very poor incouragement to set out on so dangerous a voyage, and I have reason to belive few on board, if any, would willingly go this voyage if they knowed the uncertain footing that we are going on'.

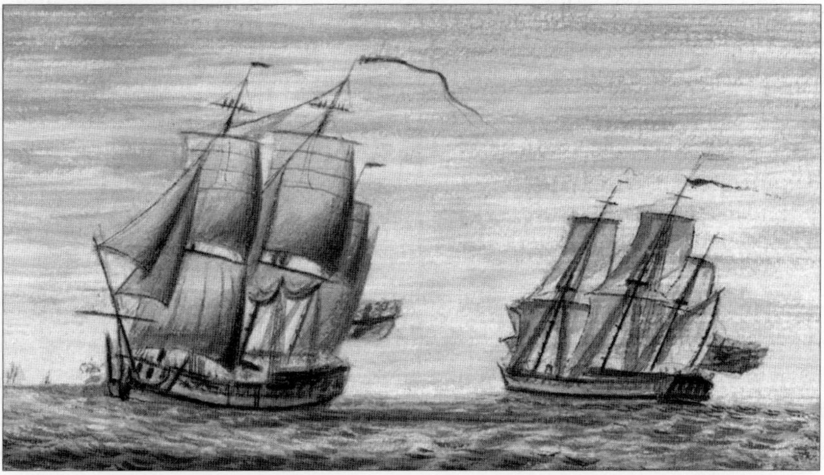

A illustration in Samuel Wallis' logbook of the Dolphin*'s voyage, now held in the State Library of New South Wales, is often said to be the* Dolphin *and* Swallow. *However, it is more likely to be the* Dolphin *drawn from two views.*

Carteret did not have the advantage of an 'Old Friend' in the Admiralty and would not learn their true destination until 13 September. There is little doubt that the increasingly vulnerable position of Egmont in the Cabinet was the reason for the downgrading of this second voyage of exploration and hastiness in the preparations, which would later prove to have disastrous consequences for Carteret. On 9 August, Carteret received orders from the Admiralty to put himself under Wallis's command and the next day he followed the *Dolphin* to the Downs and then to Plymouth. The ships set sail together for Plymouth on 11 August, but the *Swallow* was so far out-sailed by the *Dolphin* that she did not reach Plymouth Sound until the evening of 17 August, two days later. The strength of opposition in the Cabinet to the whole expedition was such that Egmont was forced to resign on 13 August. Three days later, on 16 August, before his resignation took effect, he signed secret instructions for Wallis and sent them to Plymouth where the two ships and the *Prince Frederick* were waiting. Wallis and Carteret set sail on 21 August. That Egmont had dispatched the expedition with very little time to spare is evident from a letter written by Robertson on 19 August,

> 'This day I received advice from my Old Friend that our Voyage is likely to be stopt. If we do not sail soon, but am hopefull that will not happen as we are now gone so far'.

Already smarting from his unsatisfactory exchanges with the Admiralty and the disparity between the two ships, Carteret then had to suffer the indignity of Wallis refusing his request for 2,000 lbs of junk[4]. The Commissioner Frederick Rogers, had already supplied Wallis with what he thought would be enough for both ships and as there were no further orders from the Admiralty to supply Carteret with any extra stores Wallis told him he would have to manage with the 500 lbs he had been allocated. Wallis also had on board a supply of 'trade goods', these comprised 'cloth, linen beads, scissors, knives, gimlets, saws, hatchets and other cutlery and toys' all items he would need for trading with the inhabitants of any newly-discovered lands. Previous experience had shown him that to successfully explore uncharted waters in difficult weather conditions and to cope with the unpredictable behaviour of the people they encountered, an adequate supply of both items was not a luxury but an absolute necessity. His resentment and irritation is quite apparent from the tone of a letter he sent to Wallis on 7 September when they were anchored off the Island of Madeira. The lack of junk

> 'was so inadequate to my wants, that I was in a short time after, under the disagreeable necessity, to have recourse to cut off some of my cables, in order to have those things that were requisite to preserve my rigging'.

Although Robertson, and possibly other members of the crew on the *Dolphin*, knew the destination of the voyage, Wallis had not taken Carteret into his confidence and did not reveal the objective of the voyage until 13 September when he sent the instructions to Carteret that he was to accompany the *Dolphin* on a voyage round the world and if they were separated to rendezvous at Port Famine, Chile. In his *Journal* Carteret expresses his incredulity:

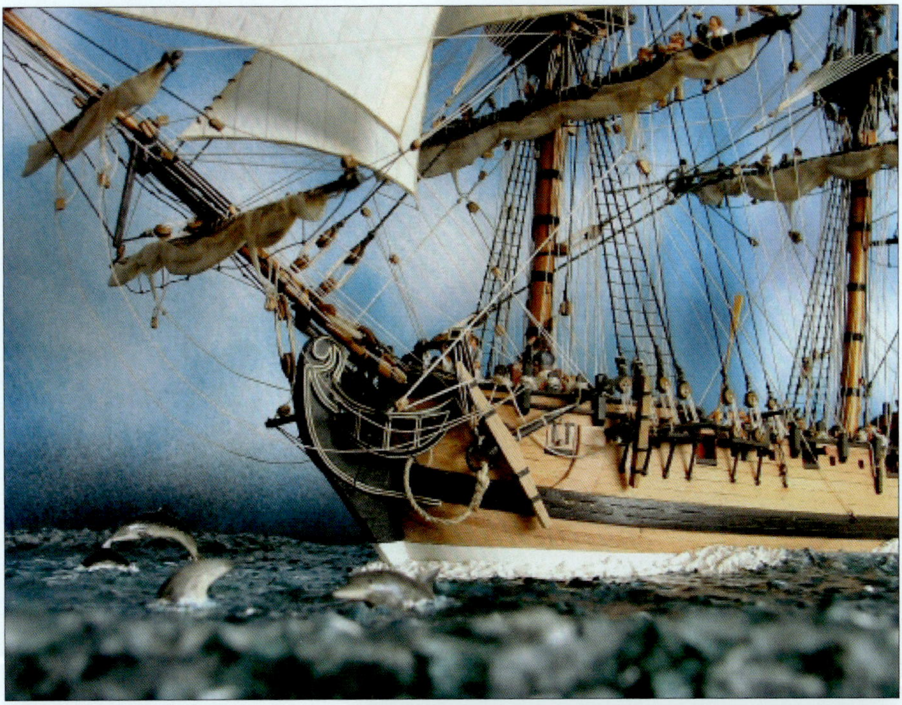

Plate 1: *Model of the* Swallow *made by Trevor Copp*
(Photograph courtesy of Doug Ford)

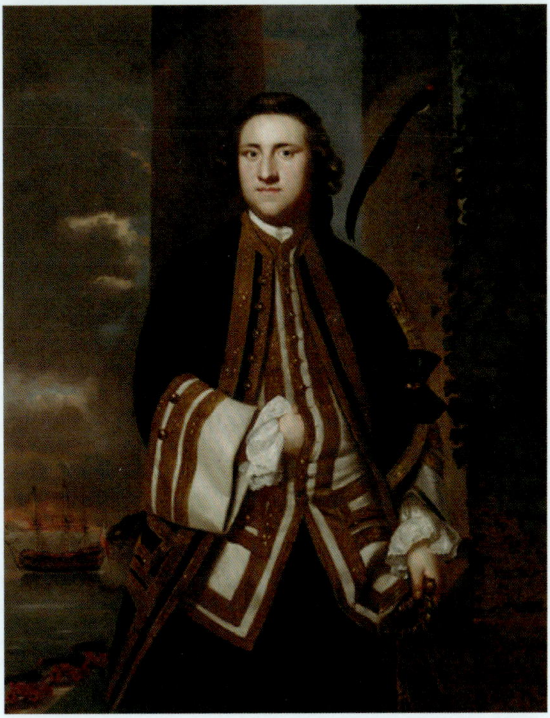

Plate 2:
Captain George Edgcumbe (1720-1795) painted in 1748 by Sir Joshua Reynolds (1723-1792)
(© National Maritime Museum, Greenwich, London)

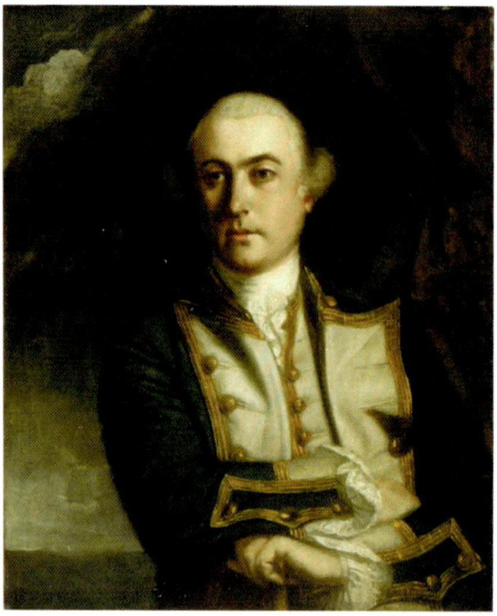

Plate 3: *Captain The Honourable John Byron (1723-1786) painted in 1759 by Sir Joshua Reynolds (1723-1792)* (© National Maritime Museum, Greenwich, London)

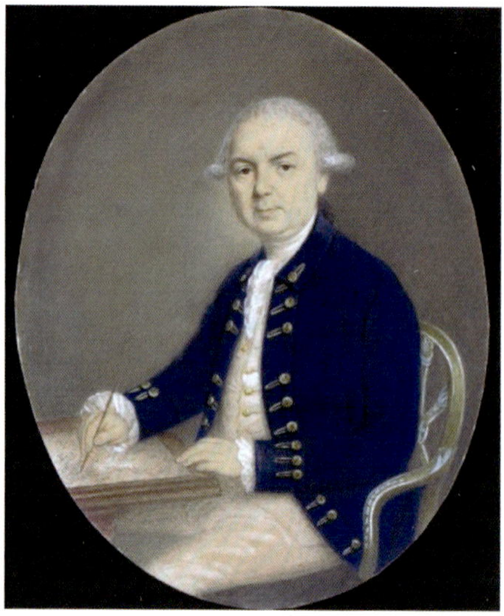

Plate 4: *Captain Samuel Wallis (1728-1795) painted around 1785 by Henry Stubble (1752-1792)* (National Library of Australia)

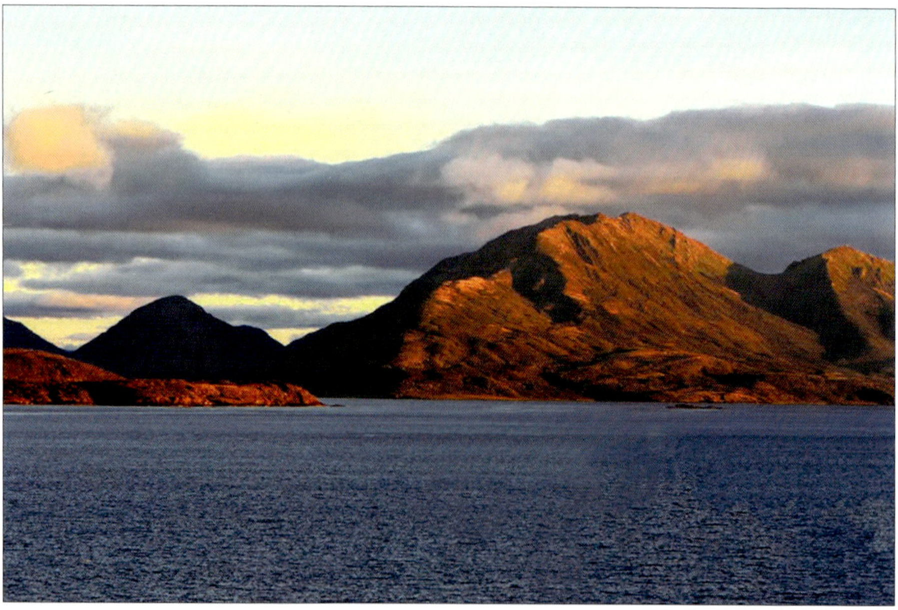

Plate 5: *Looking over to Cape Quod and the entrance to Bahía Osorno from the Strait of Magellan.* (Photograph courtesy of Doug Ford)

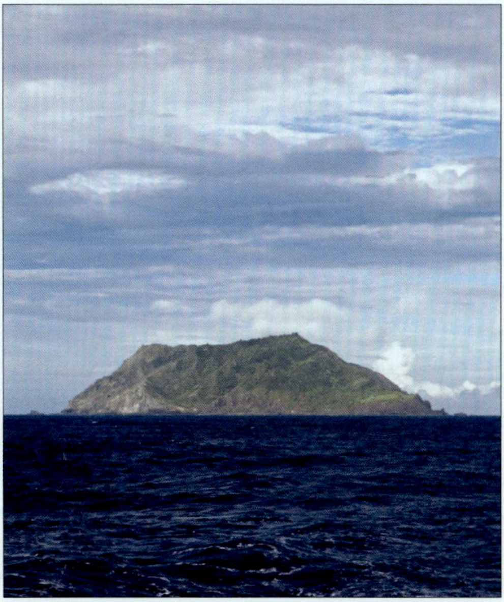

Plate 6: *Approaching Pitcairn Island from the east*
(Photograph courtesy of Doug Ford)

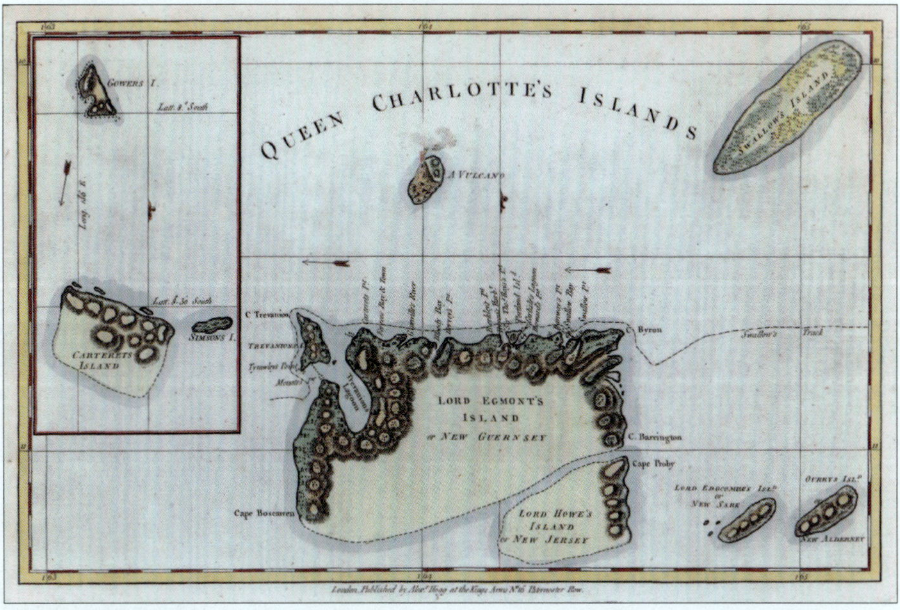

Plate 7: *Map of Queen Charlotte's Islands by Alexander Hogg (fl.1778-1819) from George Anderson's* Complete Collection of Voyages Around the World *published in London in 1784.* (National Library of Australia)

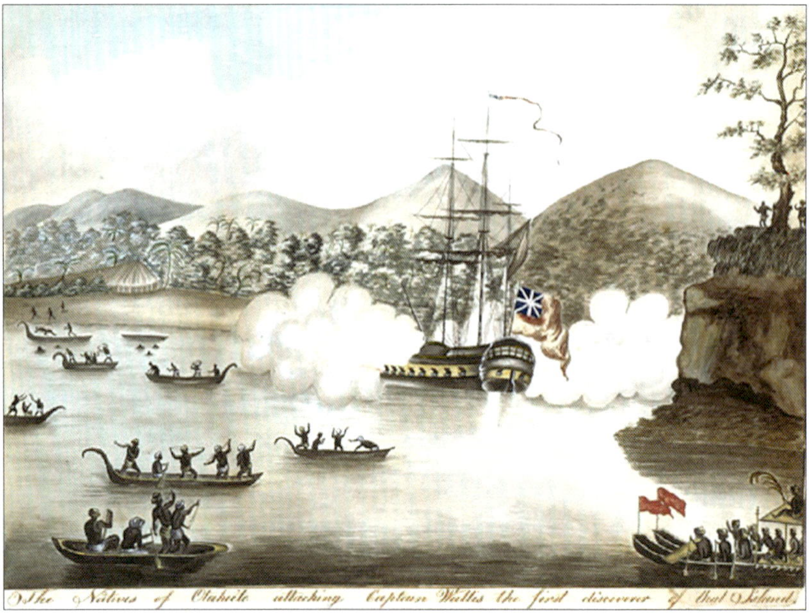

Plate 8: *The Natives of Otaheite attacking Captain Wallis, unknown artist, c.1785.* (National Library of Australia)

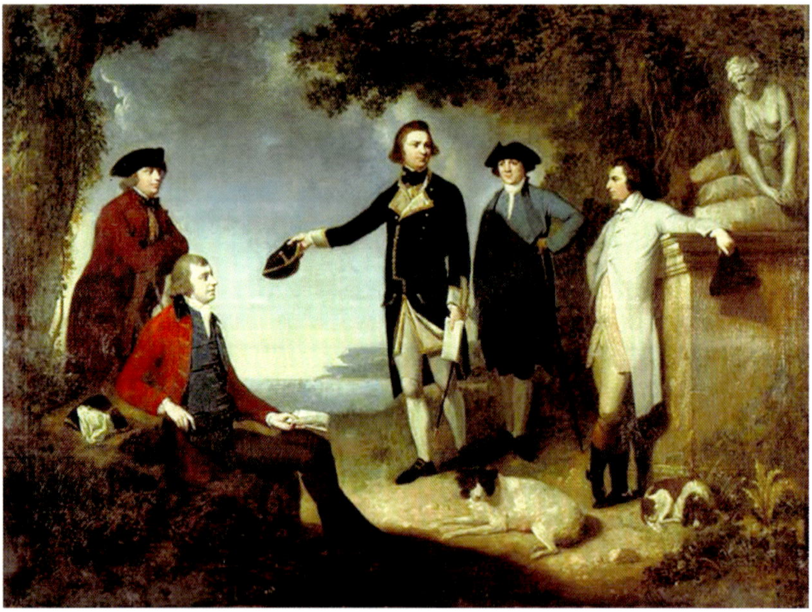

Plate 9: *Painting by John Hamilton Mortimer (1740–1779) showing from left, Dr Solander, Sir Joseph Banks, Captain Cook, Dr Hawkesworth and Lord Sandwich, 1771*
(National Library of Australia)

> 'The Reader I am certain will better comprehend, than I can write, the astonishment I was in, on perusing these Orders, & to find I was sent on a Service, to which the ill quality of my Ship, and the manner she was equipped in, made her in every respect inadequate'.

Unaware of the political ramifications of Egmont's plans, Carteret assumed that the Admiralty's calculated disregard of his interests and the preferential treatment given to Wallis was entirely due to influence, 'Nor shall I presume to inquire into the Reason, of so great a partiality for the Dolphin, or the cause of such proceedings'. He firmly believed that Wallis's patron was his former Commander-in-Chief Sir Charles Saunders, Second Lord of the Admiralty.

It is surprising that Wallis, once he had revealed his instructions to Carteret, did not consult him about the best way to execute them. The choice of a route to the Pacific was either through the Strait of Magellan or round Cape Horn. Carteret's knowledge of negotiating the former must have made it an obvious choice but it is apparent from the comment in his *Journal* that he would have to proceed 'as there was now no choise left', suggests that Wallis was determined to have total and unchallenged command over the way the expedition was conducted.

By 16 December they had reached the Strait of Magellan and the area where the Patagonians lived. The controversy over the true size of these people had raged in Europe as well as England and Dr Matthew Maty, Secretary of the Royal Society, had asked his 'good friend' Philip Carteret to make as full a report as possible on their physique, clothing, and behaviour. Carteret wrote a 'particular and certain account' whilst on board the *Swallow* on 11 January 1767. Although his original letter did not reach Maty he sent him a copy and it was eventually read before the Royal Society on 25 January 1770 and published in the *Philosophical Transactions of the Royal Society*, LX 1771.

According to his own measurements, 'they were in general all from six feet, to six feet five inches, although there were some who came to six feet seven inches, but none above that'. His evidence was corroborated by Wallis who had taken two measuring rods with him; this suggests that he had unofficial instructions from the Admiralty to establish the truth about their size. However all this careful work was spoilt by a letter written by a carpenter on the *Dolphin* that was later published in London claiming that he 'had been at the land of Giants, of whom the biggest are eight feet in height'.

Although Carteret wanted to spend more time ashore observing the Patagonians he was overruled by Wallis and the ships resumed their voyage through the Straits. It was at this point that the lack of a full complement of men began to create extra pressures for Carteret. The Master had been sick for some time and no one on board could replace him. They were about to negotiate the hazardous Strait and he was ordered

> 'to keep ahead, of the other 2 ships, in order to pilot them safely through...I had here the mortification to find how very ill the *Swallow* worked, among these Shoals, and how extremely difficult it was for us, to keep her clear from them, for it was but seldom we could make her tack, without the help of a boat to tow her round'.

By the evening of 26 December they reached Port Famine and Carteret endeavoured to improve the *Swallow's* rudder by fixing a piece of wood to it. Stores were taken on board from the *Prince Frederick* and it left on 16 January for Port Egmont in the Falkland Islands.

The alterations to the rudder had not worked and the poor handling of the ship had become such a problem that Carteret sent a letter to Wallis on 22 January in which he stated that 'we at no time can depend, on her staying or wearing' and he could no longer 'answer for the safety of my Officers', Carteret suggested that the *Swallow* be sent home with the sick. If Wallis needed him because of his knowledge of the South Seas he 'would willingly give up the *Swallow* and continue as a lieutenant on the *Dolphin*'. Wallis refused on the grounds that his instructions clearly stated that he had to proceed with both ships. Carteret's increasing frustration and desperation with the situation was such that he even suggested that Wallis should take the *Swallow* back to England and 'let me have the *Dolphin* (whose goodness I knew) I made no doubt but I should be able to fulfill the intention of the voyage'. Both men refused to compromise, Carteret's arrogant attitude towards his senior officer and Wallis's determination to stick rigidly to the instructions he had received from the Admiralty created an atmosphere of mistrust, which could only intensify.

The discrepancy in performance of the two ships resulted in endless delays and it took 115 days (twice as long as it had taken Byron) before the two ships approached the western end of the Straits and the Pacific Ocean. Robert Molyneux, the Master's mate, was sent on board the *Swallow* on 16 March and in his opinion the ship was

> 'not Calculated for a Voyage of this kind as in all Probability we should have been through the Straights before this...she cannot stow a sufficient quantity of provisions...for more than 12 months, and then for a Long Run they would be short of water.'

Bad weather kept the two ships in Upright Bay[5] from 17 March until 10 April. At 10 a.m. on the 11th, both ships were clear of the Bay. Carteret kept ahead as before, but found that the *Dolphin* sailed faster with only reefed topsails than the *Swallow* did with nearly all her sails set. At 6 p.m.when they had the western entrance to the Strait open before them, the *Dolphin* was nearly abreast. Soon after dark the *Dolphin* was seen to set her foresails and she shot ahead. By 9 p.m. Carteret had lost sight of her as she did not show any lights. She was so far ahead by 7 a.m. the next day that only her topsails were visible above the horizon and he could see that she had her studding sails set. Two hours later she was out of sight and he did not see her again.

At this point the two ships were separated by the turbulent seas of the western entrance and the weather had become in Wallis's words 'thick and dirty'. Despite all his endeavours Carteret 'could not keep up with her'. Robertson's entry for 11 April explains how the studding-sails and a fresh breeze had enabled them to 'get so far ahead of the poor dull *Swallow*'. Once the ships were separated the distance between them increased rapidly; it became more difficult for Carteret to catch up and too dangerous for Wallis to attempt to go back. The next news that Carteret had of the *Dolphin* was on 18 January 1768 when he reached Celebes[6].

Chapter 4

Abandoned

That Carteret firmly believed that Wallis had deliberately deserted him and had intended to do so from the very beginning of the voyage is apparent from an entry in his Journal:

> 'I was now fully convinced, from many circumstances which had happened from the time we left England, till the present, that Captain Wallis never intended to be troubled with the *Swallow*, after he had been safely piloted through the Streights'.

Despite his protestations, Carteret must have realised that both men actually benefited from the separation. Freed from the constraints of sailing with an ill-matched consort, Wallis kept the command and initiative in his hands and Carteret could fulfil his ambitions and make his name as an explorer in own right.

From the very beginning Carteret seems to have felt that Wallis did not share his own dedication to exploration and that he had failed to exhibit the intellectual curiosity that was one of the essential qualities required by the leader of such an expedition. Helen Wallis, the editor of Carteret's *Journal*, believed that as both men had motives for desertion,

> 'the separation was neither purely accidental nor calculated, but something half way between, an accident which neither man resisted too strenuously.... This theory also explains Carteret's attitude to the separation: his annoyance and, equally, his determination to continue alone. Although genuine in his resentment, he regretted not the fact of separation but the manner of it'.

Carteret's conspiracy theory, that the failure to give him the extra junk and trade goods and to have arranged a rendezvous point once they had left the Magellan Strait, was part of a devious, premeditated plan does not fit with Wallis's character. Wallis was not a callous or coldly calculating man and, unusually for that time, was extremely solicitous about the health and well-being of his men. His management of the men's diet and hygiene was exemplary, making sure that the ship was washed everyday with vinegar and that the men regularly aired their hammocks. Such was the high morale of his men or, Dolphins, as they called themselves, they praised him when they returned to England for the 'humane and generous treatment we have so often experienced since we had the happiness to be commanded by you.' Helen Wallis concluded that 'the episode appears as the final act in a drama not of deception but of increasing impatience and misunderstanding between honourable men'. It also revealed an aspect of Carteret's character that was destined to cloud his future career in the Royal Navy:

> 'His grievance against the Admiralty and against Wallis seem to have twisted his judgement, for it was the defect of his qualities that when he thought himself wronged he became obstinate and difficult and put the worst interpretation on other people's motives'.

When it became obvious that they would not see the *Dolphin* again the men became very dejected and Carteret gave them a morale-boosting speech in which he urged them to 'show our King and Country that we are equal to any Undertaking'. They had reason for concern, the *Swallow* had only 24 tons of water and no means of collecting fresh water and many of the men had 'ailing complaints having been greatly fatigued'. He decided to sail to the Juan Fernandez Islands off the coast of Chile for supplies, as they were 'the most convenient and best refreshing place.' However since his previous visit with Byron, the Spanish had seized the islands and he was forced to withdraw to Masa Fuero where he encountered 'an uninterrupted series of danger, fatigue and misfortunes' as the exceptionally dry summer there had ended in a series of great storms. He left the island on 25 May without taking on adequate supplies and, like many who had sailed the route before him, was attracted northward to the trade wind region 'for there is no such thing as to make the ship go or do anything without a strong wind'.

On 31 May, realising he was in the vicinity of the uninhabited islands of San Ambrosio and San Felix, he hoped to claim them so they could be used by English ships as an alternative port of call to Juan Fernandez. He was, however, misled by an error in their position on John Green's chart of 1753 and did not find them. He continued his search until 7 June when he was in 28-degrees south latitude and 112-degrees west longitude, a position that brought him close to Easter Island. It was still the depth of winter, the sea continually ran high, the winds were violent and variable and the dull, foggy cold weather was accompanied by thunder, rain and snow. This 'thick dark hazy cold' weather hid the sun for many days. Although the tricky atmospheric conditions would have made the sighting of Easter Island difficult, he noted in his *Journal* that the large flocks of birds and clumps of seaweed 'made me conjecture we were near, or had passed by some land'.

However, the adverse weather, his own weariness and the stress of knowing that his crew were on the point of running out of supplies did not deter him and he continued to sail in a westerly direction on a course more southerly than that sailed by previous navigators. To encourage the men to look out for land, the sailors were offered 'a reward of a bottle of Brandy', if it was one of the two midshipmen the land would be named after them. That honour fell to 17 year-old Robert Pitcairn who spotted a massive volcanic island (see Plate 6) rising out of the ocean 'scarce better than a large rock' on the evening of 2 July. As it was remote, uninviting and impossible to land on because the surf 'broke upon it with great violence' it was considered of little consequence at the time. (On his return to England, Robert joined the East Indiaman *Aurora*. She left the Cape of Good Hope September 1769 for India but was lost off the coast of Madagascar).

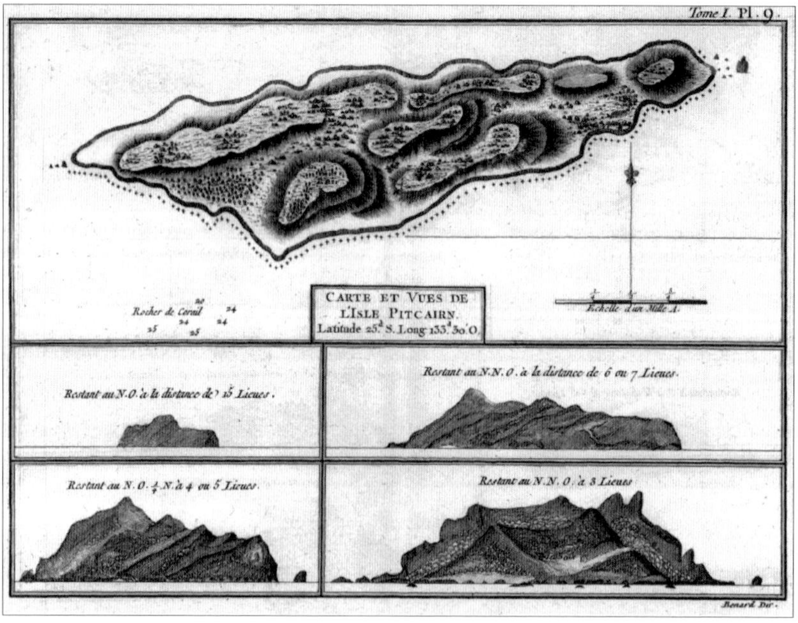

A map and views of Pitcairn Island produced by Robert Bénard as published in Paris in 1774. (© National Maritime Museum, Greenwich, London)

Thirty years later when Fletcher Christian and his band of mutineers from the *Bounty* needed a hiding-place, Christian remembered he had read an account of Carteret's discovery in a book belonging to Captain Bligh on the *Bounty* and he reckoned that Pitcairn would make a perfect bolthole. Without a chronometer to calculate longitude, Carteret had charted the island at 25 degrees south 133 degrees 21 west of Greenwich and although the latitude was reasonably accurate the longitude was incorrect by about 3 degrees (during the age of sail this equated to about two days of sail under fair conditions.) Aware of the fact that Captain Cook had been unable to locate the island in July 1773, the mutineers took advantage of the inaccurate location of the island and were able to live there undetected for 19 years.

On 4 July the *Swallow* 'began to be Crazy, by her hard labouring in the high turbulent seas'. The sails needed constant repair and the rigging kept breaking, lack of fresh supplies was affecting the men and there were many cases of scurvy. In order to provide fresh water, Carteret decided to improvise. He took a canvas cloth that had been on the floor of his cabin and turned it into an awning which would collect rainwater and provide protection against the inclement weather. He could not resist writing in his *Journal* 'N.B. This had been one of these things I had asked for, while were fitting out, and positively refused.' On 11 July they discovered three unknown atolls in the Tuamotu Archipelago but again could not land. He tried to sail south again but on 22 July, in 18 degrees South, he was forced to give up hope for the present of sailing any further in that direction. Worsening scurvy amongst his men meant he could not afford a slow passage with contrary winds.

He concluded from the course he had followed so far that 'no continent lay anywhere near' although

> 'our track...has been in as high, if not higher South latitude than any men, before which have gone across this Ocean except it be the *Dolphin* who in probability is a great ways to the Southward of us'.

It was the Portuguese navigator Pedro Fernandez de Quiros who believed that the small islands scattered around this area of the Pacific, the atolls of the Tuamotu Archipelago, were evidence of the existence of a large continent. The islands were marked on John Green's chart of 1753 but when Carteret sailed to the south of them and found nothing he concluded that there was no evidence to support Quiros's theory.

The adverse winds, increasing sickness and the damage the ship had sustained made it imperative to follow a route from which he was most likely to obtain provisions and make repairs and so Carteret

> 'judged it hazardous if not impossible to be effected in our Circumstances without imprudently running in the most eminent danger, and without the least reasonable hope or probability to meet with Success, in this so late Season of the year'.

Nearly all the victuals had been consumed or were tainted and half the crew were on the sick list when another emergency arose, a leak was reported just below the waterline. By 10 August the *Swallow* was leaking so badly the pumps had to be manned night and day to keep her from sinking.

Carteret believed, like Byron before him, that the legendary Solomon Islands, first discovered by the Spanish explorer Alvaro de Mendana in 1568, did not exist. Thus, when he saw the *'Queen Charlotte Islands'* (see Plate 7) on 12 August he did not realise that the largest island, which he called Egmont Island, was actually Santa Cruz where Mendana and Quiros had attempted to found a colony in 1595. The island had not been seen by another European since that date. If he had realised that Egmont Island and Santa Cruz were one and the same he could have followed the track taken by Quiros, plotted on Green's chart, and it would have taken him to Gracios Bay in the well-inhabited western part of the island. Instead Carteret anchored in the first available bay on the north-east coast, a wild, uninhabited area where dangerous currents impeded his attempts to mend the *Swallow's* leak. He needed to reconnoitre the coast to find a safe anchorage but instead of going himself in the *Swallow* or the cutter, he decided to send the master Simpson with a party of 15 men. Although he gave Simpson,

> 'very perticullar Orders and directions for his conduct...to run no maner of risque to be well on his guard...to be very carefull in his conduct and beheavour not to give the inhabitants any Umbrage'

his decision not to lead the party himself was to have dire consequences.

Sending a landing party to a strange coast was a very risky undertaking and had been a cause of a disagreement between Wallis and Carteret in December the previous year. After Wallis had successfully led a landing party in Patagonia, Carteret had been anxious to make another when a group of three or four hundred men were seen on the sea shore a few days later but Wallis had forbidden it because the *Dolphin* and *Swallow* were at too great a distance from the shore to protect the boat should the party get into any difficulties. Carteret was 'chagrined' at this decision as he felt they had lost 'a very fine and favourable opportunity of knowing more of them, and their country' but it is apparent from the entry in Wallis's log that his overriding concern was for the safety of his men.

Carteret's belief that the *Dolphin* must have pursued a more southerly course than the labouring *Swallow* was not in fact the case. Although the *Dolphin* was laden with stores and Wallis was scrupulous in his attention to the health of the men, they had begun 'to fall down of the scurvy' before they had been two months in the Pacific. Wallis had turned northward on 30 April 'as we no chance of getting west in this latitude, and the surgeon John Hutchinson was of the opinion that in a little time the sick would so much increase, that we should want hands to work the ship'. The Navy's Commissioners for Victualling department had taken great trouble to provide Wallis and Carteret with the anti-scorbutic remedies which were thought to be effective. These were dried malt (three measures of boiling water were added to one of malt, the resultant liquid was called wort), saloop (a powder made from dried orchid roots), sauerkraut (yellow cabbage fermented with salt and vinegar and then pressed) and portable soup. The *Dolphin* had 3,000 pounds of portable soup. It was a crude form of stock cube, a thick soup of offal and vegetables was boiled right down and then evaporated so it formed hard, glue-like cakes that could be reconstituted in boiling water. The remedy which really worked, the juice of lemons and oranges, had been recommended by naval surgeon Dr James Lind in his Treatise of 1753 but it was not accepted by the Admiralty and did not come into general use in the Navy until 1796.

The *Dolphin's* course was about eight degrees to the north of Carteret in the longitudes 110 degrees to 140 and it led the ship to the larger islands of the Tuamotu Archipelago and then on to the black volcanic peaks of the Society Islands. On 18 June they saw an island that had, according to Robertson, 'the most Beautiful appearance it is possible to imagine'. Unlike the bleak and barren Pitcairn Island, Tahiti or King George's Island, as Wallis called it, was an unexpected paradise of coral reefs edged with coconut palms, lush vegetation and cascading waterfalls.

Wallis, and later visitors Louis Antoine de Bougainville and Captain Cook, would not have known that the Society Islands were in turmoil at this time as the worship of the war-god 'Oro' was spread from island to island by an elite of high-born men and women called *arioi*. 'Oro' was a god of power and terror who demanded human sacrifices. Ceremonies were carried out at the *marae* (a stone temple dedicated to the ancestors) of Taputapuatea on the island of Ra'iatea, a place revered by Islanders as their homeland. One of the priests there had prophesied that new people would come to the islands in a 'canoe without an outrigger' and that 'this land would be taken by them'. When the *Dolphin* anchored in Matavi Bay on 23 June it was immediately surrounded by warriors in canoes. When they started throwing rocks at the sailors, retribution was swift and deadly. The ships' guns and muskets were directed at the canoes, killing and maiming dozens of men. Robertson wrote in his *Journal* that night:

> 'How terrible must they be shocked, to see their nearest and dearest of friends Dead, and torn to pieces in such a manner as I am certain they never held before'.

In her book *The Trial of the Cannibal Dog. The Remarkable Story of Captain Cook's Encounters in the South Seas,* Anne Salmond explains how the Islanders associated the sudden appearance of the frigate with the 'canoe without an outrigger' in prophecy. The thundering noise of the guns, the sudden spurts of fire and billowing clouds of smoke were signs of the power of 'Oro',

> 'human sacrifices were his tribute.... Red was Oro's colour, a sign of his presence; and the *Dolphin's* marines wore scarlet coats, just as the arioi wore red bark-cloth garments and the high chiefs wore the maro'ura, the red feather girdle. This great frigate, with its thunder and lightning, and its red-painted gun carriages and striped sides, must have seemed a strange version of Oro's sacred canoe, the *Rainbow*'.

After this incident all hostility vanished and Wallis was able to land his sick men on shore where supplies of fresh meat, fruit and vegetables were plentiful and the crew began the task of repairing the rigging, mending sails, caulking and painting the ship. These mundane activities were interrupted on 11 July when a statuesque lady accompanied by a flotilla of canoes was conducted on board the *Dolphin*. Wallis assumed from her stately demeanour and 'majestic deportment' that she was the 'Queen of the country'. Purea was indeed of high rank, being related to many chiefs on the islands of Tahiti, but at the time Wallis met her she was involved in a power struggle to establish her only son as the pre-eminent chief in Tahiti. Establishing the cult of 'Oro' in Tahiti was a key element in this plan and a great *marae* dedicated to the god was being constructed in Papara on the west coast of the island.

The crew of the *Dolphin* were bewitched by the island and its female inhabitants who were 'all handsome and some of them extremely beautiful'. By 22 July, Wallis was worried that there would be a breakdown of discipline if they stayed any longer and told Purea he must leave. When she wept bitterly he sent numerous presents including a cat in litter, needles and thread, cloth and ribbon, garden seeds and geese. In return she sent him large quantities of fruit and livestock. With his supplies replenished and his sick men recovered, the *Dolphin* sailed on 26 July leaving Purea with the red pennant of the ship. It was destined to join 'Oro's red feather girdle in the *marae*.

Wallis may have had plenty of trade goods which he could give to Purea but when Carteret sent Simpson off in the cutter on 13 August all he could give him was 'a few beads and other tryfling things, which by chance I happen to have by me, remains of my last voyage'. Simpson was expressly enjoined not to expose himself to danger, to return if several canoes advanced against him, not to leave the boat himself and not to allow more than two men to land at once, whilst the remainder held themselves on the defensive. Contrary to these orders he landed at a place where there were some dwellings and gave the men there the beads with which they seemed well pleased. He then made signs that they wanted some coconuts. When these were brought to them, Simpson concluded that the inhabitants were friendly and, impatient to get more, ordered his men to cut down one of the coconut trees.

He had ignored Carteret's express instruction not to antagonise the inhabitants and his gung-ho order to cut down the tree was the most provocative action he could have possibly taken. Pacific Islanders treat coconut trees as sacred and are loath even to replace an old tree with a new one. A taboo is placed on trees in preparation for a feast and it is then forbidden even to pick coconuts. In these circumstances the destruction of a tree is of concern to the whole tribe, irrespective of its ownership. Ominously 'a great number of men' gathered together. Midshipman William Rowe warned the Mate that he feared an attack but he 'stayed tryfling and delayed his time on shore till he found himself attacked by a great Number of Canoes by sea and some hundreds of men by land.' In the resulting skirmish, Simpson and seven other crew members were severely injured by arrows.

It proved to be the greatest misfortune of the entire voyage; it was essential if scurvy was to be prevented, to get fresh fruit and vegetables. Alienating the native population meant that there was now no chance of obtaining life-saving supplies. The men were almost too weak to work the ship, the master suffering from arrow wounds to his head, left arm and thigh. Gower was not well and on 16 August Carteret himself had an 'inflammatory disorder' that made him so ill he was confined to his bed and 'everybody expected I could not long survive'. The officers were so depleted that the gunner, who was also ill, had to do an officer's watch. Bitterly disappointed by this turn of events,

Carteret had to continue with all the daily routine of running the ship from his bed and was not well enough to go on deck until 26 August. He informed Gower and Simpson that he would have to abandon his plan. He had hoped to restore the men to health, clean and repair the ship and if she was in good enough condition to

> 'pursue our voyage to the Southward, when the Season was fit for it; & in the interim to have endeavoured making discoveries in this track, till we had go to the main land...which I supposed could not now be far off from us'.

By the main land he meant the east coast of New Holland, the name that was first applied to Australia in 1644 by the Dutch explorer Abel Tasman.

On 16 August 1767, Carteret wrote in his Logbook that his hopes are now 'blasted and damped' and that he could no longer 'persue the voyage any farther to the Southward'. However, he had not entirely given up hope of making further discoveries and decided not to take the usual route to Batavia by way of the Ladrones (a group of islands east of the Philippines) as Byron had done but headed instead for New Britain, a part of New Guinea that had been discovered by William Dampier in 1700.

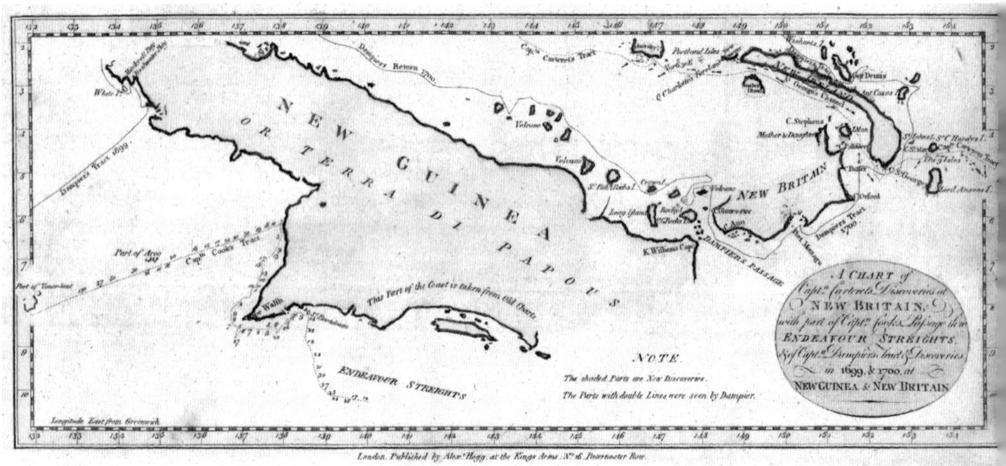

A Chart of Captain Carteret's Discoveries at New Britain by Alexander Hogg from George William Anderson's *A new Authentic and Complete Collection of Voyages*, 1784. (National Library of Australia)

Dampier had an extraordinary career. Born in East Coker, Sussex in 1651, his memorial in the church there reads; 'Buccaneer, Explorer, Hydrographer, Thrice he circumnavigated the Globe and, first of all Englishmen, explored and described the coast of Australia. An exact observer of all things in Earth, Sea and Air he recorded the knowledge won by years of danger and hardship in books of voyages and a Discourse on Winds, Tides and Currents which Nelson bade his midshipmen to read and Humboldt praised for scientific worth'.

Dampier's voyage in the *Roebuck* in 1699 was sponsored by the Crown with the instruction to explore the east coast of New Holland. He actually landed on the east coast but was not impressed with what he found:

> 'If it were not for that sort of pleasure which results from the Discovery even of the barrenest spot upon the Globe, this coast of New Holland would not have charmed me much'.

Whilst exploring the coast of New Guinea he discovered and named the strait that divides the island of New Britain from the mainland after himself.

Poring over Dampier's charts and accounts of his voyage, Carteret had been impressed by his assertion that he had found rich provisions in St George's Bay in New Britain. On 20 August at 10.30 in the morning, a small island was sighted which was named after Lieutenant Gower and to the south, two more islands appeared which they named Carteret and Simpson. Discouraged by the apparent hostility of the natives they did not go ashore or 'trouble to examine them'. Carteret was unaware of the fact that he had actually made an important discovery; these islands were part of the northernmost fringe of the Solomon Islands and had not been seen by a European since Alvaro de Mendana's expedition in the 16th century. For the *Swallow,* exploration was now no longer an end in itself, all efforts had to be concentrated on finding fresh provisions for the ailing crew. It was a heavy price to pay for the misjudgement he had made at Egmont Island. Instead of discovering the Great Archipelago of the Solomon Islands, lost for two hundred years, all he added to the map was an isolated group of three insignificant islands.

Chapter 5

Homeward Bound

Turning westward, the main voyage of exploration was now over, and the *Swallow* followed the route on Dampier's map. The misfortune that befell the expedition on Egmont Island continued to have calamitous consequences. On 22 August seaman Samuel Smith died and he was followed by marine James Fogarty on 25 August. Losing these 'two strong, stout healthy young fellows' could not have come at a worse time. Seaman Matthew Wright wounded by an arrow in his right knee died on 2 September (the ill-fated Simpson finally succumbed on 18 September). Midshipman William Rowe had also been wounded 'in the middle and forepart of the Thigh, the Arrow having broke against his bone, & the wound having heald, he continued to do his duty, till our Arrival in England'.

Three days later they sighted New Britain and looked for a convenient place to anchor. Not only was Carteret desperate to find fresh food for his crew, 30 were extremely ill with scurvy and the rest 'were but weakly', but repairs also urgently required attention. The leak had reappeared and the ship's bottom needed to be cleaned. They anchored for the night in the 'deep Bay or gulf' which Dampier had called St George's Bay, hoping to find a 'fitter place for our purpose' the next day. The parlous state of the crew was apparent on the 29th.When they tried to pull up the anchor 'we were so weakly manned' the anchor got stuck and it took hours of intense effort before they could pull it free, only to find it was

> 'disabled and unserviceable. They went and anchored in a very convenient little Cove about 3 or 4 miles from here, where we wooded, water'd and took in very good shingle ballast, and got what little refreshments we could from the Chief was Coconuts. Carteret found that the milk or rather water of these Nuts is excellent and perhaps the best Antiscorbutick that is in the world the Cabbach part of this tree is a white juicy crispy substence which has much of the taste when eaten raw of our chestnuts'.

Experimenting with this vegetable they found what when it was boiled it was better than turnips and it could also be cut 'into small strips and boiled in the broth made from our cakes, and this broth, afterwards thickended with oatmeal furnished us with a good meal'.

When Carteret went ashore he recognised nutmeg trees, palm trees, bamboos and canes but was very disappointed that he could not find 'any kind of eatable vegetable' amongst the dense and unidentifiable vegetation growing near the shoreline. During their stay in the cove he had hoped to improve the diet of the men but this proved to be an exasperating and fruitless task as attempts to entrap turtles and catch fish in the clear waters of the rocky beaches were unsuccessful. They did find a few oysters and cockles at low tide and a tree called the Jamaica plum which, 'from their pleasant tartish taste is very agreeable to the Scorbutick'. The carpenters tried to deal with leaks as best they could by coating the wood with pitch and warm tar mixed together but when they inspected the ship they found that the sheathing was greatly worn, the keel quite gnawed away by worms. English Cove, as Carteret called it, was the first real port of call since leaving the Magellan Strait. It was therefore the place to formally declare possession and a plaque was fixed to a tree on 7 September.

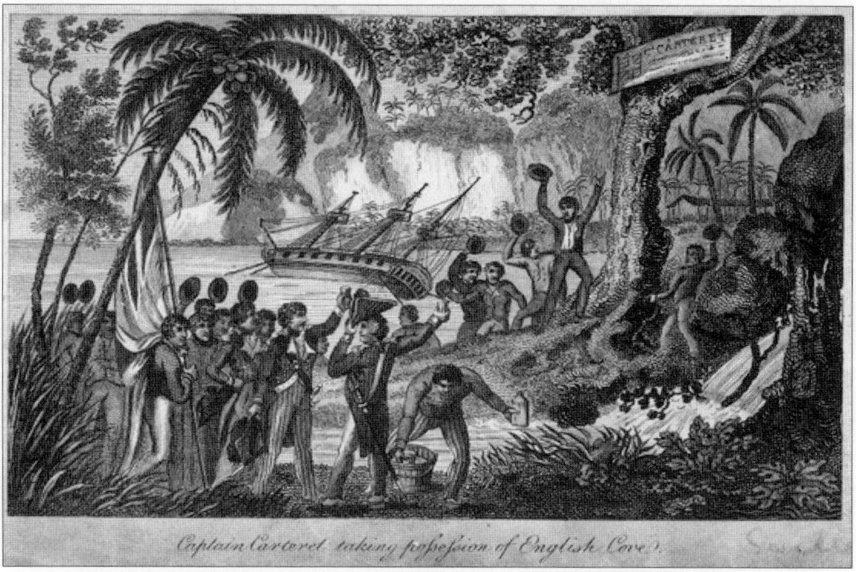

Captain Carteret taking possession of English Cove. Illustration from Hawkesworth's An account of the voyages....Southern Atmosphere, *1773*

(© National Maritime Museum, Greenwich, London)

> 'We nailed a piece of board on a high Tree on which we engraved the English Colours, Captain and Ships Name, time of coming and sailing from and Name of the Cove.'

Carteret would have liked to have stayed longer but he 'dreaded too much the consequence of being caught by the West monsoon short of Batavia in such a miserable tool of a ship', so he left on 9 September taking a thousand coconuts and a small amount of cabbage with him. The south-westerly current he encountered whilst navigating St George's Bay led him to suspect that the Bay was really

> 'a fine large Channel or Straight clear of all danger as far as I saw, so that instead of this being only an Island, I found it to be two fine islands, with several smaller ones about it, the Northernmost I named Nova Hibernia and that which is to the Southernmost and biggest retains its name Nova Britannia'.

He foresaw that this discovery would provide a useful route for merchant shipping and this was the case after Port Jackson was settled in 1788. During the season of the south-west monsoon it became the recommended route from New South Wales to India and China. He felt that a ship would be able to get provisions from the inhabitants in exchange for

> 'iron tools, beeds, Ribbens, looking glasses, pieces of Cloth linens and Showy things all which they seemed very fond of, Now I found I wanted all those things very much to traffick with the people, which I would certainly have provided myself with if I had thought of coming on such a voyage'.

Near a small island, which he named after Earl Sandwich, they encountered nine or ten canoes which had come from New Ireland containing about 150 men. They were

> 'the black woolly headed Negroes much like those of Egmont Island and go quite naked not a bit of covering over any part of the body except a few ornaments of their own making about their Arms and legs, but seemed to take great pride in their beard which some of them had very large ones powdered with white powder as well as their woolly heads which some had adorned with bird feathers that seemed to me off the Tail of the dunghill Cock by which it seems they have that Useful domestic bird. I know not if these people have any knowledge of fire Arms, while they were hovering about the Ship I kept every body to their

> Quarters; they keep a constant look out after our guns as if they had apprehended danger from them'.

These natives were Melanesian and were the ancestors of the present-day Papuan-speaking tribes. They made the powder by grounding down white coral, a practice that was used in many parts of Melanesia to decorate and bleach the hair; the men would carry the powder around with them in a small box. Carteret was right about the identity of the feathers, they were fastened to short sticks and then worn as hair ornaments by men of rank.

In this portion of narrative, Carteret gives more information about the appearance of these hitherto undiscovered islands and the inhabitants and their customs than previous explorers but he still feels he has to explain why he had not collected more facts. In fact he was still

> 'very sickly and ailing and not with standing I was so weak that I could scarce keep the deck, I yet was Obliged (for want of officers) to keep watch and watch with the Lieutenants, besides navigating the Ship make remarks, and other duties'.

Once the *Swallow* had cleared St George's Strait the direct route westward towards the East Indies was followed. This led to the discovery of a number of islands, named the Admiralty Islands. At six in the morning of 15 September, a number of canoes containing hundreds of men surrounded the *Swallow*, the hostile intent of the natives soon became apparent when spears with a 'kind of blueish flint' were hurled at the ship. Carteret ordered the men to fire over the attackers but when this had no effect some of his men fired at the canoes and injured a man 'yet I was not sorry for it, as I hoped that would have brought them to reason'. When they faced a second attack, his men 'in indignation and revenge, against all Indians; for the Death of their brother Shipmate fired a round shot from one of the six pounders', killing one man. Carteret concluded that they were 'a wild, fierce, savage People who could easily be subdued by our superiority with fire Armes'.

This incident, in which Carteret's moral authority and leadership was compromised by his failure to control his men at a critical moment, was left out of Hawksworth's official account of *Swallow's* voyage. It reflects badly on Carteret, for although he exhibited the intellectual curiosity, determination and tenacity needed to be a successful explorer, he signally failed in establishing friendly relations with the Melanesians in the Egmont and Admiralty islands. He believed that if he had enough trade goods both encounters would not have ended in bloodshed but it is doubtful that this was the real cause of his problems; he found it difficult to solve any problem by means of diplomacy and persuasion and was too ready to invoke the rule of force when peaceful means failed. After the disaster at Egmont Island his attitude was uncompromising. 'If I had not been ill I would have taught these people better manners to strangers', he was also quite prepared if he needed supplies not to bother trading but 'to have got them by force'.

Two small islands came into view on 19 September which had not been seen by a European since 1545, when the Spanish explorer Ortiz de Retes called them *Islas de Hombres Blancos* because of its white-powdered inhabitants. The island of Aua could only be seen from the masthead and the *Swallow* passed by the second, Wuvulu, in the night. Islanders carrying torches could be seen running along the shoreline. Carteret decided to name these islands after two of his London friends, Dr Matthew Maty (1718-1776), a Dutch physician from a Huguenot family who was the Secretary of the Royal Society and Francis Duroure, an attorney who was one of the Directors of the French Hospital in London.

On 25 September 1767, the *Swallo*w reached the Mapia islands, the eastern outpost of the Spice Islands. Unlike his other encounters with Pacific Islanders the inhabitants here were friendly and happy to barter goods – anything made of iron was particularly highly prized. Carteret wrote that he could have had anything in exchange for irons. When he gave a native a piece of iron hoop four inches long

> 'he thought himself as rich as anybody in the world, he jumped about and laught so very hearty with such a happy Countenance that I could not but sympathize with him in his joy'.

Although they were the neighbours of Papua New Guinea and the island groups they had just explored, these natives were not black but

> 'Copper colour'd (first of the Kind we have seen in these parts) fine long black hair, little beards...have fine white Teeth, go naked except the Privy parts they cover slightly with a narrow piece of fine matting, well made and featured of the common stature, very nimble and active, many of them went up our masthead faster and nimbler than our people could do'.

Carteret found it much easier to communicate with these natives. Like the Polynesians Wallis encountered, their culture was a more sophisticated one than the Melanesian.

One of them even asked permission to accompany Carteret on his voyage and in spite of all the representations of the crew and Carteret, he refused to leave the *Swallow*. Carteret finally consented and in recognition of his single-mindedness gave him the name Joseph Freewill. He was entered in the Muster book as number 111, and he died at Batavia on 11 February 1768.

Most explorers would have sailed south through one of the straits between Gilolo and New Guinea and then south-west to Batavia but Carteret ignored this direct route. His desperate need for provisions contributed to his decision to make for Mindanao, the most southerly of the Philippine Islands. Again his unconventional choice was determined by Dampier's discovery in 1686 of 'plenty of fresh meat' on the savannah in the 'Bay of Deer' in the south-eastern part of the island. On 26 October they sighted the north-eastern part of Mindanao. The log records that:

> 'All those people that had recovered of the scurvy from those trifling refreshments we had at Nova Hibernia are now laid up again, and more falling down',

but he searched in vain for the 'Bay of Deer'. A little farther off he found a watering place but the hostile demonstrations of the inhabitants forced him to re-embark. The fruitless detour to Mindanao left Carteret in a serious plight. With so many men sick and the last days of the monsoon approaching he had to take the shortest route to Batavia, through the little known Strait of Macassar between the islands of Borneo and Celebes. It proved to be a safe passage which he recommended as a new route for East Indiamen in the China Trade but it took 'a fortnight in getting about 28 leagues...we were now so very sickly and so much reduced we could scarce work the Ship'.

At this desperate stage in the voyage an unexpected drama occurred which had the result of rallying the crew and raising morale. In the middle of the night of 10 December, the *Swallow* came under attack from a small Pirate or rover who

> 'roused our drooping Spirits in attempting to board us, after miscarrying in this attempt and finding his mistake he endeavoured to get off, he fired away pretty briskly his little guns and small Armes, I imagine he found himself better answered in it than he had expected for soon after he sunk, I know not of what Nation he was of, as it was Night none were saved we had the Lieutenant and another man slightly wounded. (Gower's 'slight wound' was caused by a slug shot which entered his upper lip, forced three of his teeth back and lodged in his gum.')

On 12 December, with the onset of the western monsoon, the *Swallow* was in no condition to struggle against the wind and reach Batavia by the west, so instead Carteret set course for the Dutch port of Macassar on the island of Celebes (now called Sulawesi), the principal colony of the Dutch East Indies. The Dutch East India Company's lucrative trade with the Spice Islands was dependant on their possession of the port in Macassar, but the Company's control was limited to the town itself and the immediate vicinity. It was a volatile situation; the Dutch did not trust the King of Goa, the greatest of the native kingdoms in Celebes and one which had a long record of implacable opposition to the Dutch. When the British captured Manila in 1763 their reputation of being 'the great Captains of the World' fuelled the Macassar Council's fear that the King of Goa and the King of Wadjo, an adjoining state, would enter into an alliance with the British and drive the Dutch out of the area.

When the *Swallow* anchored on the evening of 15 December 1767 it was the first European settlement they had visited since leaving the Cape Verde Islands on 27 September 1766. In all, 246 days had elapsed since they left the Strait of Magellan with only one adequate stop to re-provision in that time.

They had scarcely let down the anchor when a representative of the Governor of the Macassar Council, David Boelen, came on board. He was most alarmed to discover that the ship was not a merchant ship but belonged to the Royal Navy. The next morning Carteret sent Lieutenant Gower to request fresh supplies and shelter until the easterly winds returned in early May. Such was the 'terrible fright' of the Dutch authorities at the appearance of a Royal Navy warship they would not let Gower land and he had to wait for five hours in the boat in the boiling sun for a reply. When it came it was not what Carteret was expecting. He was 'ordered instantly to depart and be gone from this port not to offer to approach any nearer nor to anchor on any part of this Coast'. When Carteret remonstrated against this harsh decision two officials, the harbour master and magistrate, were told to board the *Swallow* and ascertain its condition.

They were shocked by what they saw, of the crew of 75 men 50 men were sick, 'the sight of them could not fail to raise a shudder, they were infected by scurvy to such a degree that the teeth of most men were black and swollen and their legs blue as lazuili'. Carteret showed them the body of crew member Edward Wheatley who had died that morning and explained that his life

> 'might have been saved if they had not hindered us from getting refreshments. He then asked for some lemons for his sick men, which

were brought to them and sucked out immediately'.

The officials confirmed that the water-casks were empty and the only food on board was

> 'bad salt meat and bread full of weevils. The rigging was bleached completely white and the ship was very dirty inside and on the outside, overgrown with grass, moss and shaggy vegetation, on all sides along the water-level half a foot high'.

Carteret explained that it was impossible to set sail in such a condition and that he was now so desperate he would run his ship aground unless he was given some aid. Permission was finally granted to allow the *Swallow* to anchor in Bonthain Bay, on the southern tip of Celebes where, if payment was made, 'all refreshments, water and firewood' would be available. However, a number of regulations had to be strictly observed, and the stringency of these meant that 'in reality we were no more than prisoners'.

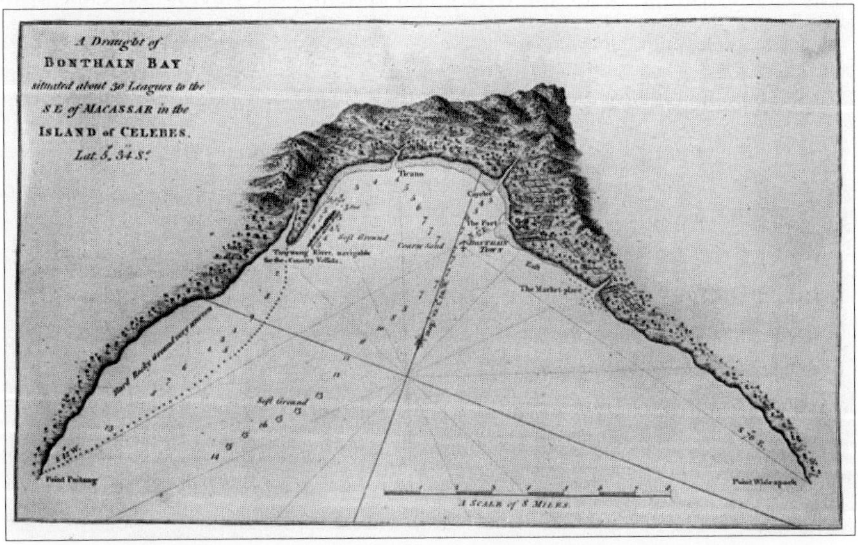

The Swallow's anchorage in Bonthain Bay from Hawkesworth's An account of the voyages...Southern Atmosphere, 1773

Arriving at Bonthain Bay on 23 December, they were allowed to use a house near the sea as a hospital and under the direction of the surgeon transferred the sick from the *Swallow*. Close surveillance of the men was maintained by a detachment of an officer, two sergeants, two corporals and 36 soldiers who ensured that no-one was allowed to move 20 or 30 yards from the hospital or let anyone on board the *Swallow* go ashore. Forbidden to communicate with local people, Carteret was unable to buy anything except through the agency of the Dutch soldiers and they abused their position by shamelessly overcharging. Fuming at this humiliating treatment, Carteret was deeply disturbed on 29 March when he received a letter, which contained 'a Warning of a plot to attack the *Swallow*'.

The letter had been written by Nicholas Ray, an Englishman who was staying in Lagoesi, a village in Wadjo. Ray was a junior employee of the East India Company, a fluent speaker of Malay and Buginese (the language of the Wadjoese). The Company had sent him to Pasir in Borneo, a Wadjoese trading centre, to negotiate a deal with Arou Matoa, the King of Wadjo, for 100 cases of linen and cloth 'of the first sort'. A revolt in the town forced him to flee with Matoa to Wadjo. There his movements had been closely monitored by the Dutch who were relieved to discover that he spent all his time hunting and 'drawing mountains, estates gardens, houses etc' for Matoa and Dato Soping, the chief of Soping. The letter, written on behalf of Matoa, explained that the Dutch had hatched a plot with the son of the King of Boni, whereby he would attack the *Swallow* with 800 men. He would be given the ship as a prize but the Dutch did not want their involvement in this action 'to be known, they are afraid to be seen in it, tho' they supply them with Powder, Ball, Ammunition etc.' A postscript conveyed an offer from Dato Soping, of facilities for an English settlement on the coast of Celebes.

Writing in retrospect, Carteret stated that he had not believed everything in the letter; however, at the time he behaved as if he believed every word. Suspicious by nature he had already been alarmed by the appearance of two merchant ships from Macassar lying close to the mouth of the river. Believing it was 'Necessary and Prudent to provide against the worst' he armed the men, loaded the guns, fixed four swivel guns on the quarterdeck and did everything he could to give any would-be attackers 'a proper reception'.

Ray's involvement in this affair was part of a complex intrigue set up by the Wadjoese designed to entangle Carteret in the local politics of Celebes. Their ultimate aim was the overthrow of the 'despised and detested' Dutch, they were the intended victims, not Carteret. The *Swallow's* unexpected appearance in Celebes gave the King of Wadjo and Dato Soping the opportunity to pursue the second rung of their plan, an alliance with the British. Ray, who appears to have been an innocent pawn in these machinations, came on board the *Swallow* on 14 April. Wearing English dress he was able to slip past the Dutch guards who assumed he was one of the crew. Ray told Carteret that the King of Wadjo was 'very desirous to put (his country) under the Protection of the English ... and offer to assist them in settling in any of these part where there is a sea port'. Carteret gave him a present for the King a 'Quadrant, books & Charts of Navigation in return for all the intelligence he had given me, with thanks for his kind offers in favour of my Country'. If Carteret had been endowed with a more temperate personality he could have exploited a difficult situation to his advantage, profiting from the intelligence that Ray offered without antagonising the Dutch but, instead of defusing the tense atmosphere on board ship, he made the situation worse by adopting a confrontational and aggressive attitude.

Although the attack never materialised, and an official of the Dutch East India Company convinced Carteret on 25 April that the 'abominable plot' to storm the *Swallow* was a complete fabrication, he never formally withdrew his accusations against the Dutch. He resolutely refused to show them the letter or reveal the identity of the person who wrote it. Boelen's private correspondence, translated from the Dutch, makes it clear that the 'despicable project', which had so disturbed Carteret, was so preposterous he thought Carteret had invented it and the letter was a figment of his imagination.

When Boelen wrote to Carteret on 27 April that he heard he had a 'Complaint of something you have heard which has made you Uneasy', Carteret's reply on 10 May was vituperative, railing against the treatment he had received from the Dutch and complaining that they had compromised his honour as a gentleman. His letter was so 'shot through with bitings and fierce expressions' that Boelen was quite dumbfounded, 'what he wishes to convey in this preamble is a mystery to us'.

When the *Swallow* finally sailed for Batavia on 22 May, the Dutch were extremely relieved to be rid of the 'ill-natured Englishman'. There had been mistakes on both sides. Boelen's initial reception of Carteret had been harsh and it predisposed Carteret towards enemies of the Dutch, however, he mishandled the situation badly. He may have come to Celebes 'not particularly well disposed towards the Dutch...but innocent of any deliberate plan to harm them. He left Celebes their bitter enemy'. His parting shot to Sergius Swellengrebel, the Dutch resident who oversaw the *Swallow's* stay in Bonthain, was the threat that he would know where to go with the facts of the plot. By this he meant Leadenhall Street, the headquarters of the East India Company. He submitted a detailed report to them in October 1769 and so set in train a sequence of events which ultimately led to the Dutch being ousted from Celebes.

Chapter 6

'Meritable but unnoticed Voyage'

There were further repercussions from Carteret's ill-fated stay in Bonthain Bay when he reached Batavia on 3 June 1768. The Governor General there had already received a report dispatched on 29 April by Boelen about Carteret's behaviour in Celebes As a result he did not respond with the customary hospitality which had been accorded to Byron and Wallis. When he received a letter expressing the 'hope' of being granted liberty to refit the *Swallow* and replenish her stores the Governor chose to dispute the use of the word *hope*. Playing for time they were in no hurry to help him. They were more concerned to secure Ray's letter and find out who had been involved in the plot. But when it became apparent that Carteret was not going to hand it over, he even denied the existence of the letter (presumably to shield Ray), they reluctantly agreed to help him. The Dutch were still investigating the affair in Celebes some three months later. A deposition to the Council of Justice at Macassar stated that 'The Captain was completely eaten up with prejudice, and continued to persist in imagining the danger which he believed himself exposed to'.

If *Swallow* was to make the return journey to England it was vital that repairs were made. Dutch carpenters confirmed that the ship was leaking and that

> 'the whole ship is unserviceable, inside and outside and in their opinion it was a very unfitt ship to go home to Europe. Carteret was worried that if they opend her bottom they might find her still worse … and so bad that they might condemn her'.

To avoid this outcome carpenters spent from 24 July to 16 August patching up the ship by placing new sheathing over the rotten timbers. The sick on board were taken to a hospital where eight men died. Another man died in an accident and William Kerton, who had sailed on Byron's circumnavigation, was left behind in the hospital. Carteret's low opinion of the Dutch was confirmed when he recruited

> '21 good English Seamen, who took their opportunity to run away from the Dutch ships, and came onboard of me; Claiming my Protection, as English Subjects. They told me they had been Kidnaped in Holland, as many others are of Different Nations'.

Once he had a full complement, Carteret was anxious to get away for 'this is a most unhealthy place, they reckin 25 hundred Europeans die here every year'.

On 25th September, the *Swallow* set sail for the Cape of Good Hope, during the two-month journey his fears about the stay in Batavia proved to be true. The crew were 'very sickly', seven men died and there were only '18 officers and men in each watch'. This stage of the voyage home from the East Indies was notorious for illness. 'The flux' (tertian malaria and dysentery) was an infection caught from the contaminated water and provisions, which were taken on at Batavia. When they finally reached the Cape there was an immense feeling of relief. Everyone 'breathed a good air, had the wholesome food, & went freely about in the Country which is extremely pleasant, & I began to think my self already in Europe'. Unlike his experience in Celebes and Batavia, Carteret encountered 'good manners, an open polite behaviour, a hearty welcome and honest Hospitality'.

'Well refreshed' they left the Cape on 6 January 1769, stopping at St Helena where Carteret wanted to find out whether Europe was at peace or war, and then on to the uninhabited Ascension Island. Here they caught 18 turtles 'all from 4 to 6 hundredweight each'. Before leaving the Island they complied with the custom 'for all ships to leave a letter in a bottle, signifying their having touched here; we ...took a Copy of those letters, we found in it'. On Sunday 19 February, a ship flying French colours 'out sailed us much'. During the night she had turned around and by noon the next day 'she was near enough to hail us, they called me and the Ship by our proper Names'. Greatly surprised they were asked how they could identify them and the reply was that they had called in at the Cape of Good Hope a few days after the *Swallow* and there they had read in the *Gazette de France* about the disappearance of the *Swallow* and the assumption 'that we had been ship wrecked in the Straits of Magellan'. The ship was the *Boudeuse*, a 26-gun frigate under the command of Bougainville. He had left Nantes on 15 December 1766 with the store ship *Etoile*, with instructions from King Louis XIV to find the 'unknown southern continent'. After handing his settlement in the Falkland Islands to the Spanish he had followed a similar route to Wallis and arrived in Tahiti in April 1768 where he stayed for ten days. Like Wallis before him, he was preoccupied with controlling his men when they encountered the beautiful young women of the Island, 'I ask you, how was one to keep four hundred French sailors, who hadn't seen women in six months, at their work in the midst of such a spectacle'.

By a bizarre quirk of fate Bougainville landed in the same cove in New Ireland where the *Swallow* had anchored 11 months before:

> 'A sailor, belonging to my barge, being in search of shells, found buried in the sand, a piece of a plate of lead, on which we read these remains of English words, HOR'D HERE .... ICK MAJESTY's. There yet remained the mark of the nails, with which they had fastened this inscription, that did not seem to be of any ancient date. The savages had, doubtless, torn off the plate, and broke it in pieces'.

They found the tree which the plate had been nailed to and the place where the crew had pitched their tents. Bougainville was sure that it was the *Swallow* as

> 'We have since heard of this ship at Batavia ... and where it will appear, that we from thence followed her track to Europe. This is a very strange chance, by which we, among so many lands, come to the very spot where this rival nation had left a monument of an entreprize similar to ours'.

Bougainville was determined to catch up with the *Swallow* and find out what he could about their voyage. He called in at Ascension Island on 4 February, three days after Carteret had left it, and from the message in the bottle learnt of the latter's visit:

> 'He arrived here the 31st January, and set sail again on the first of February; thus we had already gained six days upon him after leaving the Cape of Good Hope. I inscribed the *Boudeuse*, and sent back the bottle'.

As Bougainville did not want to reveal the fact that they were also on a voyage of circumnavigation a young officer was sent on board the *Swallow* with the story that the *Boudeuse* belonged to the French East India Company and they had been on a trading voyage to Sumatra. Carteret was suspicious because the officer was 'drest in a waistcoat and trousers; whether he was drest in this unofficer like manner, with any design or not; I will not pretend to say'. He felt that 'this gentleman's questions and pert enquiries, rather extraordinary, but had here unto only attributed them, to the Natural Curiosity of Frenchman'. Offering, on behalf of Bougainville, 'all the services that one may render to another at sea' Carteret thanked him but said he did not require anything and gave him an Indian arrow to give to his Captain. Whilst this exchange was going on, Dominic Pane, the *Swallow's* quartermaster, who was born in French-speaking Quebec, spoke to one of the French sailors, who could not resist bragging that 'we have been round the Globe as well as you'. Carteret was mortified when Lieutenant Gower told him this after the ships had parted company.

Bougainville knew that he would reach Europe before 'poor dull' *Swallow* and when the *Boudeuse* arrived at St Malo on 16 March he sent a letter the next day to Pierre-Jacques Mesle de Grandclos, an extremely wealthy merchant and ship owner who had made a huge fortune out of the slave trade. Mesle lived in the Manoir de la Baronnie, on the outskirts of St Malo. He sent the letter containing the news that Philip was *en tres bonne Sante* to his friend *Monsieur de Carteret, Chez M.Gosset a Jersey*. Richard de Carteret was a cousin of Philip and was also a successful ship owner and merchant. The address presumes that he was staying with his brother-in-law Matthew Gossett of Bagot Manor. Richard forwarded the letter to the Admiralty with a covering letter dated 23 March explaining that the enclosed had been received the day before.

In fact the *Swallow* had docked at Spithead on 20 March. Carteret immediately dispatched a letter to the Admiralty reporting his return and the main events of his voyage and the observation that the *Swallow* 'was perhaps the worst ship that could have been pitched upon in all his Majesty's Navy'. He explains that he cannot leave the ship as his gunner and boatswain Richard Campbell are very ill (he died on 5 April) and Midshipman William Rowe was also ill, the arrow which had entered his thigh had broken up 'and came all out at the gartering place, near the Ham, having worked themselves down so low'. He received a reply from the Admiralty Secretary, Philip Stevens, the next day instructing him to present himself at the Admiralty Office in London with 'the Abstract of your Voyage...Journal and Log Book...Charts, Plans and Drawings', and the logbooks and journals of the Officers and Petty Officers.

Much had happened during the 31 months the *Swallow* had been at sea. Saunders, Wallis's patron, had only lasted as First Lord of the Admiralty for three months and had been succeeded by Admiral Sir Edward Hawke on 11 December 1766, so when Wallis and Carteret returned they no longer had the backing of the one man who might have secured for their men some recognition of their sufferings and achievements. When Carteret was fretting in Batavia about the repairs to the *Swallow's* rotten timbers, the wharves and piers of the Royal Navy Dockyard at Deptford had been a hive of activity as preparations went ahead for the Navy's most ambitious and well-equipped expedition to the South Seas. Led by James Cook who, unusually for the time, had 'come in through the hawse-hole', a hand-picked group of naval officers, the botanist Joseph Banks, his entourage of five servants, the naturalist Daniel Solander, the astronomer Charles Green and two artists were about to embark on the first of three epic voyages of discovery. They would ultimately produce a comprehensive map of the Pacific Ocean and record unprecedented information about the 'Genius, Temper, Disposition and Number' of its inhabitants and flora and fauna.

James Cook had served under fellow Yorkshire man Hugh Palliser at the siege of Quebec. Following the Treaty of Paris, Cook was given the task of surveying and charting the coastline of Newfoundland and from 1762 he had worked on a set of charts which delineated the coastline with painstaking precision. Palliser actively supported this work and assisted in the publication of his acclaimed map of Newfoundland. When a dispute arose over the extent of the fishing rights in the area, Cook's expertise brought him to the attention of Lord Egmont, First Lord of the Admiralty. Egmont was immediately impressed by his exceptional skill as a surveyor and cartographer and by his interest in astronomical observations (his account of an eclipse of the sun in Newfoundland in 1766 had been published in the Royal Society's Philosophical Transactions). The Royal Society had decided that astronomical observations should be made in the South Pacific to record the moment when the planet Venus crossed the sun in 1769, as it was hoped this information would help determine the size of the solar system. The King agreed and granted the Society £4,000 to cover expenses. A Whitby cat[1] was purchased by the Navy Board and re-named the *Endeavour*[2]. Not only was Cook familiar with this type of ship, he had learned to sail on them. He also possessed the diverse skills required to lead such a complex and high-profile expedition. Philip Stephens, the Secretary of the Navy, put his name forward for his patron Palliser who supported the post but, before he could receive a commission, Cook had to sit his lieutenant's exam.

He received his commission from the Admiralty on 25 May 1768, five days after the arrival of the *Dolphin*. Although the crew had been sworn to secrecy their discovery of Tahiti soon became common knowledge and a song extolling its virtues could be heard in the inns and taverns of London:

'Then we plow'd the South Ocean, such land to discover
As amongst other nations has made such a pother.
We found it, my boys, and with joy we it told,
For beauty such islands you ne'er did behold.
We've the pleasure ourselves the tidings to bring
As may welcome us home to our country and King.

For wood, water, fruit, and provision well stor'd
Such an isle as King George's the world can't afford.
For to each of these islands great Wallis gave name,
Which will e'er be recorded in annals of fame.
We'd the fortune to find them, and homeward to bring
These tidings as a tribute to country and King'

The information gathered by Wallis added a new dimension to the enterprise. Thanks to the involvement of the Royal Society the Royal Navy now had another chance to search for the 'great Southern Continent' and six crew members of the *Dolphin* volunteered to join the *Endeavour*. One, Charles Clerke, promoted to master's mate, had also sailed on the first voyage under Byron. It was reported in the *Gazette de France* that the *Endeavour* would be visiting Tahiti; the inclusion of this destination led the French to assume that another objective of the expedition was to find out what had happened to the *Swallow*. The *Endeavour*, 106 feet in length and 29 feet wide, was tightly packed with all manner of supplies, animals, astronomical and botanical equipment, trade goods, guns, ammunition and provisions for 18 months at sea when it set sail on 26 August 1768. Cook wrote in his journal,

> 'At 2 p.m. got under sail and put to sea having on board 94 persons including Officers, Seamen, Gentlemen and their servants'.

His first set of instructions from the Admiralty was to proceed to Tahiti to observe the Transit of Venus, the second set ordered him to search for the unknown continent,

> 'whereas there is reason to imagine that a Continent or Land of great extent, may be found to the Southward of the Tract lately made by Captain Wallis in His Majesty's Ship the *Dolphin* (of which you will herewith receive a Copy)'.

Despite the much-vaunted discovery of Tahiti the hard-headed Lords of the Admiralty were not prepared to offer any financial reward to the officers and crew of the *Dolphin* when they returned to England. A letter written by George Robertson on 24 June 1766 shows that he believed they would get the same financial award or 'Incoragement' as Byron's crew had done (double pay and other advantages) but six weeks later he discovered it would be conditional on the discovery of 'a Place of Consequence in the South Seas'. The crew asked Wallis to present a petition to the Admiralty to determine whether this was the case and so resolve their 'state of uncertainty'.

The reply in June 1768 was negative and their only recompense was that 'suitable notice' would be taken of the men 'with respect to promotion'. Embittered by this response, one of Wallis's crew was so disillusioned with 'service under his own nation' he sold information about the voyage to a spy in the French and Spanish embassies and offered to transfer to the service of Spain. Wallis was just as disenchanted. He wrote that all he had gained from the voyage was 'much ill health and fatigue'. He had been so ill when they got back to England 'he could scarcely stand'. Still ill after a year (his symptoms suggest pulmonary tuberculosis), he had run up heavy medical expenses and petitioned for recompense. In 1770 he was granted a two-year leave of absence and a gratuity of £525. In 1782 his financial situation was further bolstered when he was made Extra Commissioner of the Navy, a post he held until his death in 1795.

He fared better than Carteret who, at the age of 59, suffered a 'paralytic Attack brought on by the Hardships he had undergone when <u>twice</u> Circumnavigating the Globe' but he never received a gratuity. When the *Swallow* was finally paid off at Deptford on 17 April, the muster roll had 31 DD entries (Discharged Dead). Carteret asked that benefits be paid to those men who had been severely incapacitated by scurvy. They included Thomas Lesk, a carpenter who had lost one hand and 55 year-old John Renshaw who was recommended for his 20 years' of service as the *Swallow's* carpenter.

Carteret also wrote recommendations for Lieutenant Gower, 'I am deficient in words to do him Justice', the surgeon Thomas Watson and the purser Edward Leigh. When Watson asked for compensation for his 'extraordinary expenses and services in looking after the sick at Bonthain Bay' his claim was dismissed as 'there was not any thing particular in the disorders of the men at Celebes'. However, he did receive an allowance of 6s 8d for each man he looked after at Batavia. (The surgeon on the *Dolphin,* John Hutchinson, was treated in a similar manner, his expenses totalled £125.5.6 but he only received £30 from the Admiralty.) As for the *Swallow,* the Admiralty considered that the repair bill of £1,181.17s was too high and she was sold at Deptford for £545.

Similar promises of immediate promotion 'uniformly held out to all' had been made to the crew of the *Swallow* but as the months slipped by and these promises were not fulfilled, Carteret and his officers became increasingly bitter about the Admiralty's ingratitude and disinterest. Edward Leigh wrote to Carteret on 19 January 1770:

> 'There is going to be, so is the talk, of a great change in the Admiralty and that Your Friend Lord Egmont will succeed Sir Edward Hawke and if so, to speak without flattery I most sincerely wish You will be in some measure Gratified for Your imminent Risque and indefatiguable trouble and perseverance on our late merittable but unnoticed Voyage'.

When the position was filled a year later it was not Lord Egmont but Lord Sandwich, and during his ten years of tenure of the office, he was no more helpful to Carteret and his men than Hawke had been. It is apparent from Leigh's reply to a letter which Carteret wrote in the spring of 1770 that he was very critical of the Admiralty, 'it shews the true Sentiment you have of their behaviour'.

Carteret's naval career had so far been dependant on the 'interest' of Byron. When he wrote to him on his return Byron replied that he was en route to Newfoundland where he would take up the post of Governor for three years. It is apparent from Gower's letters to Carteret that another 'old shipmate', a Lieutenant John Ferguson, was also dependant on Byron. He wrote in November 1774 that he was seeking command of the *Cherokee*[3], a ship that 'was worth seeking for he had Mr Byrons interest, several candidates they that have least interest of course will go to the wall'. Ferguson was appointed to the ship on 16 January 1775, 'Mr Byron got him the appointment, its supposed he will be able to make three hundred a year of it'. It does not appear from surviving correspondence that Carteret had any other 'interest' at the Admiralty. If he was entirely reliant on Byron he was unable to help Carteret and ten years elapsed before he received another commission.

Chapter 7

'Hawkesworth has brewed it'

When Carteret finally returned to Trinity Manor on 12 January 1770, his sister triumphantly hoisted the frayed and weather-beaten colours of the *Swallow* on the Manor flagpole. Resuming his responsibilities as a landowner and the Seigneur of Trinity, he found he was immediately involved in the dramatic power struggle which had flared up the previous year. From the time of George de Carteret in the 1660s the Crown appointment of Bailiff had been a hereditary one for the de Carteret family. However, as many of the Bailiffs were absentees, preferring to stay in England, they appointed a Lieutenant Bailiff to exercise the office in the Island. In 1750 Charles Lemprière, Seigneur of Rozel, became Lieutenant Bailiff. He was in charge of the Royal Court, the all powerful institution which both administered and wrote the law of the Island. The elected members of the State Assembly were subservient to the Court and could not pass legislation without the Court's consent. Lemprière had strengthened his grip over the Island's legal and administrative system by appointing relatives to key positions.

Lemprière's autocratic regime was challenged by his bitter enemy, the merchant Nicholas Fiott and three army officers on half-pay, Moyse Corbet, Philippe Falle and Charles Le Geyt. Fiott had been forced to flee to London from where he carried on his campaign against Lemprière. In September 1769 the *Salisbury Journal* reported that 'There are great disturbances in Jersey on account of the exportation of corn'. *A* ferment of unrest had erupted when Charles Lemprière was accused of exporting corn from the Island to create a shortage and so increase the amount of money he made from *rentes*.

Every year the important Seigneurs like Lemprière would fix the value of the *Wheat rente*. This was a local form of mortgage raised on real property – money would be lent on condition that the Seigneur received annually so many quarters of wheat. This was generally paid in kind but sometimes in money, according to a fixed scale which varied with the market price of wheat. If the price fell so did the Seigneur's income, if it was artificially manipulated to benefit the Seigneur, the prices soared and the poor suffered.

On 28 September 1769, the anger and resentment against Lemprière burst into violence when 200 men from the parish of Trinity joined protestors from other parishes and marched into St Helier demanding justice. They burst into the Court House wielding sticks 'in such a furious manner that Carteret's attorney Charles Poingdestre did not believe that any of the magistrates could escape with their lives'. The Lieutenant Bailiff and Jurats (elected lay judges) took refuge in Elizabeth Castle and petitoned the King. Colonel Bentinck was sent from England with a detachment of soldiers and instructions to restore peace and find out the cause of all the unrest. On 13 February, Carteret invited him and the leaders of the anti-Lemprière party to dinner at Trinity Manor.

Carteret actively supported the rebels, together with the political satirist and campaigner John Shebbeare, whom Fiott had persuaded to go to Jersey and produce anti-Lemprière propaganda. (Shebbeare was Le Geyt's son-in-law.) By placing himself firmly in the anti-Lemprière camp Carteret had alienated himself from the current Bailiff, Robert Carteret, 3rd Earl Granville (he held the office from 1763 until his death in 1776) and by so doing would have lost an influential 'interest'. It was widely reported that Carteret's visits to London in 1771/2 were to actively gain support for the rebels. By 1773, the Island divided into two camps, those who supported Lemprière and the *status quo* were called Charlots and those with a more outward looking and progressive outlook, initially led by Guernsey lawyer Jean Dumaresq, were first known as the *jeannots* and then *magots*.

The merchant classes of Jersey, keen to expand and develop overseas trade and bring new wealth to the Island, directly challenged the old world view based on feudalism and privilege. An aspiration which was supported and encouraged by French Huguenots who had fled from persecution in France in the late 16th century and again in 1685 when Louis XIV revoked the Edict of Nantes. For Huguenots who came from Normandy, Brittany and Poitou-Charentes, the islands of Jersey and Guernsey provided a safe haven from which to make the journey to England. If they decided to stay, they found a reassuringly familiar environment, sharing the same language, the Protestant faith and a strong work ethic. Close alliances were soon formed with local families through marriage and common business interests.

However, success for Channel Islanders in the wider mercantile world was impeded by the supremacy of the French language. If commerce with Britain was to flourish it was imperative that merchants should be able to converse and correspond in English. When the Chamber of Commerce met for the first time in St Helier in February 1768, predating similar institutions in Britain by 15 years, two of the founding members were from Huguenot families, Pierre Amiraux, a silversmith from Saumur and Jacques Hemery, a merchant and shipowner whose father came from Vidouville in Normandy. Hemery was one of the few Jersey merchants to be bilingual and it is indicative that the knowledge of both languages was seen to be so integral to the Island's future prosperity that the minutes of the first meeting were written in English. The subsequent 'Anglicisation of trade' and the rapid expansion of Jersey's mercantile and commercial interests meant that Jerseymen and Guernseymen were, by the middle of the 18th century, setting up offices in London to deal with Islanders' needs. These firms performed a number of services. They were

> 'agents for Island privateers in wartime, acted as bankers; arranged insurance for Island vessels and their cargoes; invested money in the funds for Island merchants; paid allowances for the children of Island merchants who were being educated in England and performed a dozen other useful tasks'.

The merchants were closely involved with the French Huguenot population in London. Many Huguenots had fled to Jersey after the Revocation of the Edict of Nantes in 1685; sharing the same language, religion and work ethic they were soon integrated into island life and formed close alliances with Jersey families through marriage and common business interests.

Richard de Carteret, the recipient of Bougainville's letter, worked with Carteret's 'good old friend' Jerseyman Noah Le Cras in an office in Walbrook close to Mansion House in London, the hub of commercial activity in the City. There they dealt with the complicated requirements of their clients in Jersey and Guernsey. Their ties with the Huguenot community were close. Le Cras's brother-in-law Pierre Triquet, was a partner in one of London's largest and most successful firms of master silk weavers, Ogier, Triquet and Vannsommer, which was based in Spital Square. Their shop in Pall Mall attracted an illustrious and very wealthy clientele. Richard was married to Jane Gosset. The Gossets were a prominent Huguenot family who fled to Jersey in 1685 when their title and estates in Normandy were confiscated by the Catholic monarchy. Richard's brother-in-law, Matthew Gosset, remained in Jersey and pursued a career as a merchant and ship owner but his uncle Isaac moved to London producing miniature portraits in wax and elaborately carved picture frames from his studio in Berwick Street. The business flourished; fashionable society loved his exquisitely modelled portraits, often incorporated into fine pieces of furniture, and artists like Gainsborough were happy to pay top prices for his frames. Eventually, Isaac moved to the prestigious address of Edward Street, Portman Square, and in 1774 he was appointed Royal frame maker, supplying the frames for Alan Ramsay's state portraits of the King and Queen.

In 1765, Gosset made a wax medallion portrait of Francis Duroure, a London attorney who also came from a Huguenot family. Francis was a friend of Philip Carteret (he named the island Aua in the western Pacific Ocean after him in September 1767). The Gosset family and Francis Duroure were closely involved with the French Hospital in London (Duroure was made a director in 1764, secretary 1765-1783 and deputy-governor from 1785 to 1797). 'The Hospital for Poor French Protestants and their Descendants Residing in Great Britain' was granted a Royal Charter in 1718. Called La Providence by its grateful inmates, the building on a site near Old Street in Finsbury in North London was gradually extended over the years and by 1760 housed 230 people. It 'was one of the earliest institutions in London to serve the capital's needy immigrants, and it was one of the first in Britain to provide sympathetic care for the mentally ill'.

From 1742 to 1774 that care was provided by its physician Dr John Baptist Silvester, Philip Carteret's father-in-law. Jean-Baptiste Zacharie Silvestre came from a family of distinguished physicians, forced to flee from the family estate near Bordeaux. His uncle had come to England as physician to William of Orange. An enlightened and extremely able man, John Silvester was accepted as a Fellow of the Royal Society in 1747, 'being a gentleman of Merit and Learning, well versed in Philosphical and Natural knowledge' and was knighted by George III in 1774. Prior to his appointment to the French Hospital, Silvester was physician to the British army stationed in the Low Countries and it was there that he married the Huguenot Aletta Catherine Everardina D'Aulnis de La Lande in 1740. Their daughter Mary Rachel was born the following year and on 5 May 1772 she married Philip Carteret in the church of St Stephen and St Benet, Sherhog, London.

Around 1760, Silvester had acquired a fine eight-bedroomed house near Church Street (now Mare Street) in the village of Hackney in North London. The estate had extensive grounds which included a garden laid out in the old-fashioned formal style, a brew-house, dove-house, dairy and 'farm-yard with Barn, Stable, Cow-house and 15 acres of land in high manurage'. He decided to invite a young German gardener whom he had met in Velzen in Harlem to update the garden in the fashionable landscaped style and add a collection of 'foreign shrubs'. Joachim Conrad Loddiges (1738-1826) emigrated to England to work for him and between 1762 and 1771 created a spectacular garden which contained 'two greenhouses…a curious grotto with a constant stream murmuring through…a Brook making five falls…a Gothic Hermitage…a Shrubby and Serpentine walk' and 'a fine Chinese bridge'. Its most striking feature was the display of mauve *Rhododendron Ponticum,* a species introduced from Turkey. This rare and very valuable shrub flourished in Silvester's garden and Loddiges became the first gardener to supply and distribute them, the Marquis of Rockingham becoming his first customer in 1763.

Silvester continued to care for the mentally ill in the 1770s when he and his partner Richard Devey ran a private lunatic asylum in Balmes House in what is now the De Beauvoir Estate in Hackney (Guernseyman Richard de Beauvoir bought Balmes House in 1680). When Silvester decided to retire in 1777, he purchased a house from the Marchioness of Lothian in the exclusive Royal Circus in Bath and sold his London house and estate for the substantial sum of £2,100. Loddiges then began his own business selling seeds and plants from a shop on the corner of London Lane and Church Street and later moved to more extensive premises east of Church Street, where his nursery became a major centre for the introduction of new plants into British gardens.

Carteret would have had ample opportunity to enjoy the gardens after his marriage to Mary and it is not perhaps surprising that the enterprising Loddiges realised that Carteret's observations of the indigenous plants he had seen on his travels had commercial potential. In 1783 Philip replied to Loddiges's enquiry as to whether 'the winter Cortex tree' (*Drimys winteri*) which he saw growing in the Strait of Magellan would be worth importing,

> 'The Tree is very handsom, & easily to be brought to England, as a person may Chuse from many Thousand small ones, of different growth, & Size according to ones convenience or fancy; this tree, would not only be an ornament, but of Use in this Country.... I wish you Success in getting this tree'.

Three years earlier Carteret had been asked by Sir Joseph Banks to take William Brass, the former gardener to the Duke of Northumberland, on board the *Endymion*[1] when she transported troops to Goree in West Africa so he could collect some plants there and store them on board the ship. Banks explains that he has permission from one of the Lords of the Admiralty for this mission and would take it as 'a personal favour' if Carteret agrees. Banks explained that he realised if there were 'an engagement all such lumber must be hove overboard' but he knew that under Carteret's care the specimens would be safe. As the plan to take troops to Goree and attack the French settlement in Senegal was abandoned, the subsequent fate of Brass and his plants is unknown.

Philip and Mary returned to Trinity Manor in June 1772. During the eight years they spent there, Philip failed to get a new commission and had to manage on half-pay. This was a system devised in Charles II's reign to solve the problem of the expansion of the navy in wartime and its contraction in peacetime and was intended as a 'retainer' to keep naval officers in the service while there was no employment for them. Carteret had been given the rank of post-captain in 1771, and although he had received a commission as captain of the *Flamborough*[2] in 1771, it came to nothing as the ship was written off by the Navy Board before he could take command. Not surprisingly when he heard in 1772 about a petition to Parliament complaining about the inadequacy of the half-pay system he was keen to collaborate with the instigator of the petition, Captain Michael Henry Pascal[3].

Pascal wrote to all half-pay officers for their opinions, they received 272 answers and these are preserved in Carteret's papers. The petition was presented to Parliament by Lord Howe. A committee was appointed and when it reported to the House of Lords, Howe moved the proposal for an addition of two shillings a day to be added to the full pay of captains serving in fifth and sixth rate ships as these junior officers were found to be suffering the greatest hardship. The Chancellor of the Exchequer seconded the motion and the House asked the King to consider the extra support for junior captains and commanders and proportionate amounts for senior captains. Pascal died in Southampton in 1786. The Carteret family had moved there in 1781; that they remained good friends is evident from Pascal's will, 'To my good friend Captain Carteret of the Navy residing in this town I give my uniform sword and sword belt'.

When John Montagu, 4th Earl of Sandwich was appointed First Lord of the Admiralty on 12 January 1771, he immediately took a close personal interest in Captain Cook's voyage and exploration in general. When the *Endeavour* returned to England on 12 June, the news of the discoveries made on the voyage rapidly circulated and a wave of excitement and enthusiasm was generated which spread far beyond the academic and scientific community. Sandwich and the Admiralty could only benefit by being closely associated with the principal participants and the promotion of a second voyage. Banks had met Sandwich when he left Oxford University in 1764 and – despite the

25 year difference in age – the two men had become close friends. In the same year, Banks had inherited the impressive Revesby estate in Lincolnshire, which yielded an income of £6,000 a year. It was rumoured that Banks had put £10,000 of his own money into the first voyage. On his return, Banks expressed an interest in making another voyage and it is indicative that it was Banks who informed Cook on 19 August that he had been promoted to Commander.

The next month Sandwich invited Cook, Banks and Solander to his country estate, Hinchingbrooke House in Cambridgeshire, where he unveiled an ambitious project to publish an illustrated and authorised account of the voyage as well as those made by Byron, Wallis and Carteret. He asked Dr Charles Burney, a leading figure in literary and artistic circles in London, to suggest someone to write the book. Burney suggested that Dr Hawkesworth was 'the proper person to write the Voyage' for it was felt that the 'rough draught' written by the Commanders involved was not polished or literary enough for the general public.

John Hamilton Mortimer was commissioned to paint a group portrait of five men; Banks, Solander, Cook, Sandwich and Hawkesworth (see Plate 9). In the portrait, the men stand in a clearing in a wood. Cook stands in the centre of the group wearing full dress uniform, he gestures with his hat to an expanse of water in background, in the other hand he holds a chart. Banks wears a very fashionable combination of red frock coat and brown breeches and is seated in the left foreground holding a book and gesturing towards some plants, behind him is Solander leaning on a stick. Sandwich leans against a classical statue with a air of nonchalant disdain, his polished riding boots, perfectly cut frock coat and embroidered waistcoat, the informal but elegant attire of the aristocratic Englishman relaxing on his country estate with his favourite dogs. The composition of the painting and the dynamic of the relation between Banks, Solander, Cook and Sandwich leaves Hawkesworth on the periphery looking anxious and ill at ease in a matching suit of blue, a colour and style that was out of fashion in 1771.The higher social standing of Banks and Sandwich is evident in the fact that they are bare-headed, Solander and Hawkesworth are wearing hats and Cook's gesture suggests he is saluting his employer with his.

The task Hawkesworth was given was virtually impossible. The *Voyages* was aimed at two entirely different and conflicting audiences. The literary public who wanted an erudite and polished piece of literature and a more specialised public who wanted a factual and detailed account of the voyages and discoveries. Hawkesworth, an 'ingenious and elegant writer' was blithely self-confident about the project. As ignorant of nautical matters as he was of maritime history he decided to give the material a distinctive format by writing it in the first person so that the accounts should 'more strongly excite an interest, and consequently afford more entertainment'. Fusing together the four separate accounts, changing locations and opinions and inserting extraneous reflective and philosophical digressions, resulted in a work that was admired and hated in equal measure. Horace Walpole described it as at best, 'an account of the fishermen on the coasts of forty islands' whereas another reviewer saw it as a 'real authentic Account of a new World, such as no European could have figured in his own Imagination'.

There had been an enormous controversy in the Press about the project when it was revealed that he would be receiving an advance of £6,000 from the publishers. As one contemporary remarked, it was an inordinate amount of money for 'the easy Business of a few Months, transacted by a Man's own fire-side whereas the commanders had risked their lives and did not get a penny'. The project was mismanaged by the Admiralty from the start. Hawkesworth had been assured by Sandwich that each draft he wrote would be read out to the Commanders in the presence of Sandwich and that 'such emendations as they suggested' would be made. Sandwich, who had ordered the Commanders to hand over their papers, was as cavalier in his attitude to their rights in the publication as he was with promises of promotion. Although it was his duty to safeguard their interests this did not happen and he submitted the drafts instead to a team of men who were never identified. When the three royal quarto volumes of *An Account of the Voyages in the Southern Hemisphere* appeared in May 1773 all the Commanders denied that they had been consulted and protested that it contained 'misrepresented facts'. Hawkesworth's ability to distort and exaggerate was such that James Boswell exclaimed to Captain Cook, 'Why, Sir...Hawkesworth has used your narrative as a London Tavern-keeper does wine. He has brewed it'.

The overwhelming amount of material Hawksworth had been presented with and the short time frame he was given to complete it meant that the project was not the 'easy business' he had imagined. In fact the experience had been so stressful his wife wrote that it had 'destroyed Ye Fragile Fabrick of the Body'. When the *Voyages* were published they were greeted with such a vituperative and prolonged barrage of criticism it 'broke his Heart' and he died seven months later. Fanny Burney wrote that 'I believe he has had reason to detest the fortune which only preceded detraction and defamation'.

Carteret was devastated by the coverage of his voyage. He must have hoped that at last everyone would know what really happened but every controversial issue relating to his relations with Wallis, the Admiralty and the Dutch had been played down. The exceptional difficulties which he had to deal with appear 'but imperfectly and faintly' and at the crucial moment when the *Swallow* and *Dolphin* parted company the narrator tamely observes, 'I thought myself the more unfortunate in this separation'. The absurd exaggeration of the size of the Patagonians 'more properly called giants than tall men' was given further circulation by the inclusion of an engraving of Byron dwarfed by a Patagonian. Expecting to read an objective and accurate account of his epic voyage Carteret found instead a 'poetical Romance' laced with emotive language and sentiment. Hawksworth's version of the pirate attack on the *Swallow* is typical of his effusive and flowery style:

> 'It is not perhaps very easy for the most fertile imagination to conceive by what our danger and distress could possibly be increased; yet debilitated, sick, and dying as we were, in sight of land that we could not reach, and exposed to tempests which we could not resist we had the additional misfortune to be attacked by a pirate'.

Carteret was the only Commander who wrote his own version of what happened. He undertook this 'disagreeable necessity' because he felt if he remained silent everyone would believe Hawkesworth's version was accurate and true. Intending the manuscript 'for the good of the Service, and the Security of future navigators that they may have all the observations I made, many of which have been omitted' it was not published until 1965 when Helen Wallis edited it for the Hakluyt Society. Whatever the literary critics thought of the *Voyages* it was one of the most popular publications of the 18th century. Hawkesworth may have toned down Carteret's trenchant criticism of the Admiralty but the general public's reaction was that he had been badly treated. A letter to the Earl of Sandwich, which appeared in the *Public Advertiser* in September 1773, complained that the choice of the *Swallow* and the lack of equipment was 'the most stupid, base and barbarous Appointment that can be conceived, and is a plain Proof of the little Value some Wretches set on the Lives of better Men than themselves'.

In the same year, Bougainville's *Voyage autour du Monde* was published. Carteret, still smarting from being deceived by the Frenchman, wrote that the book 'will be more amusing to the landsmen than usefull of Seamen'. He suspected that Bougainville had an ulterior motive for the voyage, which had been kept secret, and that he was 'intent on something else than discoveries'. In fact Carteret was quite right. The French Government had instructed him to make observations in the Pacific for future trade and settlement and to assess a plan for planting spice trees in the Island of Mauritius in order to eventually break the Dutch monopoly in that trade. When Captain Cook visited the Burneys in February 1772, he saw a copy of Bougainville's book on the table. 'He turned it over, and made some curious remarks on the illiberal conduct of that circumnavigator' when he met Carteret in the middle of the South Atlantic. Dr Burney asked him to point out on the map exactly where this encounter had occurred, this Cook did and then he marked out his own track.

Twelve years later, Carteret's 'true spirit of discovery' and powers of observation were celebrated by G.W. Anderson in his *A new, authentic, and Complete Collection of Voyages round the World.* Comparing the achievements of Wallis and Carteret as explorers, he found that Wallis had

> 'little of that watchful attention, curiosity, and ardent desire to catch the manners living as they rise, which were possessed by Captain Carteret, and which appear so eminently conspicuous with Captain Cook'.

He has nothing but unstinting praise for Carteret's devotion to duty and triumph over almost insuperable difficulties.

Chapter 8

'That neglected and gallant officer'

The start of the War against the American colonies in 1775 must have rekindled Carteret's hopes that he would at last receive a commission. However, the Navy was not placed on a full war-time footing until February 1778, when England declared war on France. It was to be another year before he was successful. Throughout the 1770s the need for full-time employment became even more pressing as Mary and Philip's family grew but his naval income remained the same. The couple had six children, Elizabeth Mary was born in 1774, Samuel Silvester in 1775, Philip in 1776 and Caroline in 1780, two children died in infancy.

Lieutenant Gower did not have to wait as long as Carteret for another commission, but whilst he was on half-pay from 1773 to 1775, he wrote despairingly to Carteret that 'none but people of the first interest gets on in our service now'. Although he was nine years younger than Carteret he had even considered retiring. His prospects improved in 1775 when he was made First Lieutenant on the frigate *Levant*[1] under the command of Captain George Murray. During the next five years of service in the Mediterranean he was able to amass a sizeable amount of prize money (a letter to Carteret written in 1784 mentions a sum of £5,000). His next posting also brought him an excellent opportunity to be in the thick of the action when Admiral George Rodney, Commander of the West Indies Station, appointed him as First Lieutenant on his flagship the *Sandwich*[2].

Carteret was not so lucky. Relying on his friendship with Byron, he does not appear to have gone out of his way to find an influential sponsor in political and naval circles and signally failed to be seen in a favourable light by either the Commissioners of the Admiralty or the Navy Board. The former were a mixture of politicians without naval experience, dismissed by many as being 'men bred from infancy to a quill' and professional naval officers but it was all a matter of you who you knew. Richard Pickersgill, for example, was a 17 year-old midshipman on the *Dolphin*. When he wanted to join the crew of the *Endeavour* his uncle, John Lee, got him the post of Master's Mate. Lee was a servant in the household of George Jackson, the Secretary to the Commissioners and he put in a good word as a favour to his employee. The Navy Board looked after the administrative affairs of the naval service, the building and repair of ships and the supply of provisions but Carteret failed to curry favour with that department as well and, as Helen Wallis pointed out, 'he seems to have antagonised them through his importunity and persistence'.

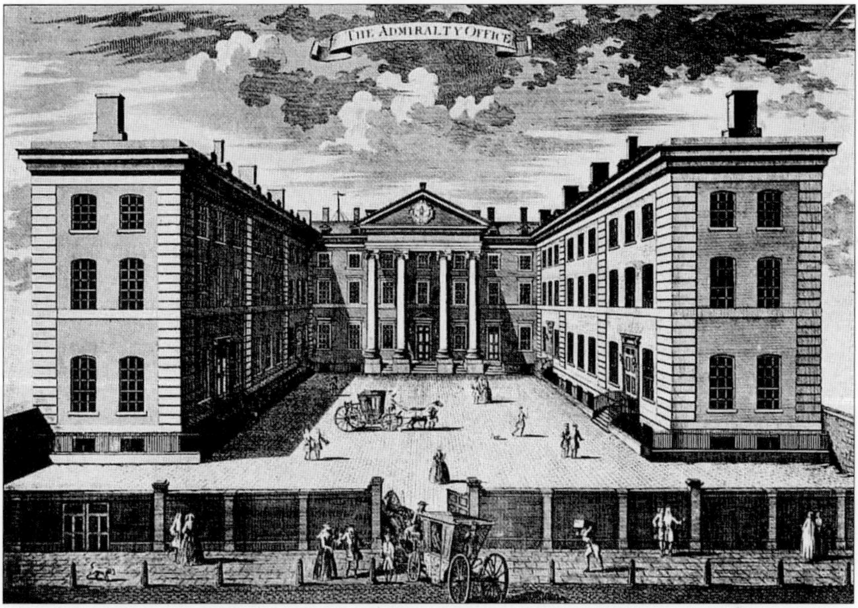

The Admiralty Building c 1760 by Domenico Cunego (1725-1803)
(UK Government Art Collection)

During this difficult time Carteret made 'repeated offers' of his service to the Admiralty and made 'close personal attendance in daily expectation of employment'. The journey from his father-in-law's house in Hackney to the Admiralty building in Whitehall must have been a depressingly familiar one. Built in 1726 on a site that was bordered on one side by St James's Park and on the other by Spring Gardens, it was the first purpose-built office building constructed in England and the 11-hour day worked by its staff the longest in any government office. It is little different today than it was when Carteret entered the courtyard from Whitehall, the stone screen of classical pillars enlivened by a pair of columns topped with a hippogryph and a panel of dolphins. The facade of the building is dominated by a portico of four Ionic columns that rise through three storeys to a pediment decorated with the carved cartouche of the Admiralty. On either side of the courtyard are two wings that contained housing for the First Lord, the Commissioners and other officials (some of the old link extinguishers remain attached to the entrance doorways).

The waiting area in the hallway would have been a crowded and noisy place filled with naval men of all ranks anxiously waiting for the call to the inner sanctum on the first floor, whilst innumerable clerks carrying rolled up charts and maps and piles of documents scurried from office to office. The entries in Carteret's Diary for August to December 1778 give a vivid picture of what a demoralising and time-consuming business it must have been waiting for an interview with either the First Lord or the Secretary, Philip Stevens. A staircase led off from the hall to the state rooms, offices and the oak-panelled Board Room which still contains the long mahogany table round which the First Lord, Commissioners and First Secretary would be seated. Over the fireplace a pair of exquisitely carved festoons frame a wind-dial showing the seas surrounding England bristling with allegorical figures.

23 August	*went to Kensington and Dined at Mr Duroure...*
28 August	*was sent for to ye Admiralty*
16 Sept	*went to Mrs Matty*
19 Sept.	*went to ye Ady. but could not see Mr Stephens.*
21 Sept.	*spoke to Mr Stephens at ye Admiralty about the Pomona*[3]*, to be launched today at Southampton he told me that she was given away to Captain Waldegrave so that my hopes there are over....*
9 October	*waited on Lord W---- nothing favourable*
16 October	*went to speak to Mr Stephens*
26 October	*went to ye Ady.*
26 November	*went & spoke to lord Denbigh who promised to speak to Lord S. about a ship etc.*
28 November	*went to Lord Denbigh who told me he had spoken to Lord Sandwich who had assured him that I should have a ship & that he would provide for me & his Lordship Denbigh assured me he would at all times assist me with his Interest etc.*
30 November	*went to ye Ady. & waited all the day without doing anything......*
1 December	*went to ye Ady. Spoke to Mr Stephens & waited till ye evening without an Answer from Lord Sandwich.*
2 December	*Went to ye Ady. Spoke to Lord Sandwich*

16 December *Received a letter from Mr Le Gros about a note he had received from Mr Stephens of ye Ady.*

20 December *...this evening I got Mr Le Gros letter from London by way of Bath but none from Mr Stephens*

The Diary shows that Carteret's tedious routine was interspersed with a visit to the two friends whose name he had given to islands in the Pacific. Like his father-in-law, they came from a Huguenot background and were learned, professional men who were Fellows of the Royal Society. Mrs Matty could either be the widow of Dr Matthew Maty, who was made a Fellow in 1751 and was Principal Librarian of the British Museum until his death in 1776, or the wife of his son Paul Henry who continued with his father's job at the Museum and was a Fellow and then General Secretary of the Royal Society. Matthew Maty was one of the men who supported Duroure's application to become a Fellow in 1774, citing the fact that he was 'well versed in several branches of literature'. Duroure was an attorney with an office in Throgmorton Street and a house in Kensington, an area that at that time would have been in the countryside.

It also reveals that he had found someone who had promised that he would 'at all times assist me with his Interest'. Basil Fielding, 6th Earl Denbigh, was a Gentleman of King's George III's Bed Chamber and a member of the Privy Council and so would have been in an influential position in political and court circles. Another useful contact which Carteret had made by this time was Field Marshall Henry Seymour-Conway. He had been Secretary of State, Northern Department in 1766 when preparations for Wallis's voyage were made and in 1772 he became Lieutenant-Governor of Jersey. (In 1780 Conway and his wife were godparents to Philip's daughter Caroline.) His older brother Francis, Earl Beauchamp was Lord Chamberlain from 1766 to 1782 (he lent Carteret his copy of Bougainville's *Voyage autour du Monde*). On 1 August 1779 the seemingly endless years of lobbying finally paid off and Carteret was given command of the 44-gun frigate *Endymion*.

After repair to damage caused by a gale, the ship was ready for service in the spring of 1780, under orders to intercept a convoy expected at Cherbourg and with the approval of the Admiralty he detained a neutral Danish ship, the *Mathia*, which had a cargo of deals and spars. In his papers he states that he was ordered to pay £870 costs and damage and there is no evidence he ever recovered this sum. Worse was to follow. Originally ordered to take troops to Africa for an attack on a French settlement in Senegal, the plan was abandoned and he was ordered to sail on to the West Indies – he arrived at Barbados on 17 September 1780. On 5 October he was caught in a fearsome hurricane whilst sailing between Dominica and Martinique. The *Endymion* was badly damaged losing a mast. In the ensuing chaos Carteret was nearly killed by a severe blow to his head. Along with the *Egmont* and *Suffolk* they were 'obliged to go to Jamaica in distress'. Five other Royal Navy ships were wrecked or foundered and three others were so damaged they were forced to return to England for a refit.

When the news reached Jersey and England of the devastation wrought by the hurricane in the Leeward Islands, Carteret's family and friends feared that he must have been killed. It was not until early the next year that Mary found out that in fact Philip had arrived in Port Royal, Jamaica on 30 October. Many letters of condolence to her and later ones of congratulation on his survival are amongst his papers in the National Maritime Museum Archive.

Once the *Endymion, Egmont,* and *Suffolk* were repaired, they joined the *Grafton, Trident* and *Bristol* under the command of Admiral Sir Peter Parker in Port Royal, the operational base of the Royal Navy in the West Indies. They were facing a French fleet of 20 ships-of-the-line, which had sailed from Brest in March under the command of the Comte de Grasse. On Wednesday 2 May 1781, Carteret recorded in his logbook that he gave chase and captured two ships. They turned out to be the *Rebecca* and *James* which had sailed from Liverpool with supplies for the beleaguered British Army in New York but had been captured by the French privateer *Franklin*. Thirty-two prisoners were taken on board and then transferred to the *Suffolk*. An even bigger prize was captured by the *Endymion, Suffolk, Trident* and *Bristol* on Friday 4 May. The *Marquis de Lafayette*, 32 guns, an old French East Indiaman loaded with vital arms, ammunitions, uniforms and general supplies for the Americans, had left the port of Lorient in Brittany on 29 March bound for the rebel-held port of Boston. The ship was escorted by the American frigate *Alliance* which was commanded by the fearless John Barry[4], (he later became known as the 'Father of the American Navy'.) Three days out from France the *Mars*, a privateer from Guernsey, and the *Minerva* from Jersey made a foolhardy attempt to attack the convoy. The *Alliance* destroyed the *Mars'* rigging and although badly damaged the brig was repaired and sent to Philadelphia under an American crew.

A prize crew from the *Lafayette* took over the *Minerva* with orders to follow the *Mars* to Philadelphia, but the French captain secretly ordered his men to take the prize to France should the chance arise. On the night of 18 April the

Minerva slipped away and a week later the *Lafayette* became separated from her escort in a ferocious storm. Ironically the *Alliance* had sighted the Royal Navy convoy on 2 May but had managed to avoid them. The *Lafayette* was not so fortunate. Carteret's entry in his logbook for 4 May shows his close involvement in the action,

> 'At quarter past 12 within half gun shot of the chase. Began to engage. At half past 2 his Maintop mast being shot away and his top yard obliged the enemy to strike'.

The *Endymion* had been relatively unscathed in the action, one sailor had been killed, the rigging had been damaged and there were 'shot holes in the sails'.

However, proper repair to the 'masts and yards' which had been damaged by the hurricane and a spell 'in Dock to repair her Copper' had to be done in England. Carteret was ordered to bring her home, sailing in charge of a convoy from Jamaica with the captured American prizes. Whilst he had been fighting the French and the Americans in the Caribbean there had been a dramatic and dangerous turn of events in Jersey. When France joined the war against Britain, Jersey privateers had exacerbated the delicate balance of power between themselves and the French by intercepting French mercantile shipping and even operating in support of the Royal Navy off the coast of America. The disruption caused by the privateers and the substantial losses that were sustained led the French to mount an unsuccessful invasion of Jersey in 1779. It was followed in January 1781 by another attempt when a French contingent of 1,000 men landed at La Rocque. Unchallenged they made their way to St Helier where they were defeated in a pitched battle in the Market Square (now the Royal Square) by the Island militia and British garrison.

For those Islanders who were out of the island and were waiting for news it must have a difficult time. Dr Daniel Dumaresq wrote to his sister Elizabeth de Carteret who lived in St Ouen's Manor,

> 'I only knew of your danger by vague rumour which gave me the greatest anxiety...I heard that the enemy troops had been dispersed and had been totally defeated'.

Mary Carteret decided it was time to leave Jersey and move to England, The family's furniture and maid were sent to Southampton and arrangements were made to transfer money from Jersey to London. Mary stayed in London from March to May 1781 with John Meyrick, a wealthy magistrate who owned a house in Great George Street, Westminster, and Peterborough House, a splendid mansion set in twenty acres of grounds in what was then the village of Fulham. By this date her father had moved to Bath and her brother John was progressing in his career as a lawyer (he became Recorder of London in 1803 and was made a baronet in 1814).

To finance the family's move to England, Trinity Manor was leased to the British Army for use as a barracks. The agreement which initially ran from 13 June to 27 August 1781 brought in a guinea a week, but when it was extended the arrangement brought Carteret further expense. The soldiers vandalised the property, the banisters were burnt, windows broken, table linen destroyed and the carefully tended walled garden and 'promenade' garden became a wilderness of weeds. In September 1781 there was a sale of the contents of the outbuildings on the estate as well as an 'old horse called Juno', 10 lambs and 31 sheep. This was followed in October by a sale of furniture which made a total of approximately £16 sterling. The family's choice of Southampton for a new home was not surprising. The town had traded with the Channel Islands since the Middle Ages and had flourished during the 18th century when the Island's production and export of knitted woollen stockings brought wealth to the merchants who had settled there. Many Jersey families sent their children to school there, as it was a cheaper alternative to Winchester College. During the second half of the century it was discovered by English 'persons of rank' and it gained a reputation for being a smart resort and spa town with a Circulating Library and Assembly Rooms. The High Street where the Carterets resided was 'One long fine street of a quarter mile in length' containing 'shops that rival the metropolis'.

The sizeable Jersey community there included merchant Clement Hilgrove, the brother-in-law of Matthew Gosset. Both men joined Noah Le Cras and Richard de Carteret in various business enterprises, the most ambitious being the purchase in 1774 of the ship *Venus*. The total cost of the ship and its fitting out to go to the Bay of Honduras to bring back a cargo of mahogany came to £5,971.10s 3d.sterling (the V*enus* was captured by an American privateer in 1778.) Clement became Mayor of Southampton in 1778 and again in 1789. Another business associate and relative by marriage, Thomas Durell, was Mayor in 1790 and in 1795 it was General James d'Auvergne, Philip d'Auvergne's uncle. Hilgrove's accounts show that he obtained and sent all manner of commodities to Jersey. Carteret's accounts show that the miscellany of items, which were sent from Jersey to Southampton, included the local newspaper, powder for wigs, pots of honey and barrels of oysters.

Philip finally arrived back in England at the end of October. He was completely stunned when he was informed that he would be paid off and his ship given to someone else. One can only imagine Carteret's state of mind on 3 November when he visited the Admiralty and wrote a letter to Sandwich. It is apparent from the letter that Sandwich had made it plain he did not want to speak to him, 'yesterday was much disappointed and shagreened (as your Lordship saw company) in being excluded that honour'.

His situation was now worse than before as the injury sustained during the hurricane meant he was unfit to be sent on service overseas so he requested command of the *Cambridge*[5] which was being fitted out for home service. Sandwich replies that he will see him at 11 the next morning but nothing came of the meeting. Carteret never lost his belief that the Royal Navy was the 'great (nay the first) Department in the public line' but it was a very overcrowded profession. Between 1771 and 1782 (excluding 1779) Sandwich received nearly 3,500 applications for promotion or favour from Lieutenants, Masters and Commanders and Post captains. He wrote to Lord Berkeley that:

> 'The Candidates for promotion in the Navy are so numerous that it is absolutely necessary for me to hold the same language to all who address themselves to me upon that subject, and I am obliged to have the most strict attention to the seniority of those who either by themselves or friends sollicit preferment'.

If, on the other hand, the applicant had the right 'interest' and was of the correct political persuasion a request for 'preferment' was speedily dealt with. In 1763 when Egmont was First Lord of the Admiralty, Augustus John Hervey (later Admiral and 3rd Earl of Bristol) asked Sandwich to use his influence on behalf of Captain Paul Henry Ourry. Ourry (1719-83) was the son of Louis Ourry, a Huguenot refugee who had settled in Jersey in 1724 and had been a lieutenant on the *Salisbury* when Carteret joined the ship in 1747. When Carteret discovered the island of Vanikoro in the Santa Cruz group he named it after Ourry but this was altered in Hawkesworth's account where it appears on the Chart as New Alderney. Sandwich wrote:

> 'I'm very glad to hear you give so good an account of Captain Ourry's political disposition, in consequence of which if he will apply for a guardship at Plymouth I am well assured he will meet with success, and have one of the first ships that is commissioned'.

We learn from a letter from Gower to Carteret in 1775 that Ourry had been given the lucrative job of Commissioner of Plymouth Dockyard:

> 'I suppose you will be surprised to hear that Commissioner Rogers has quitted his post at Plymouth, and that Paul Ourry has suceeded him'.

(There is a portrait by Sir Joshua Reynolds of Ourry with his black servant at Saltram House.)

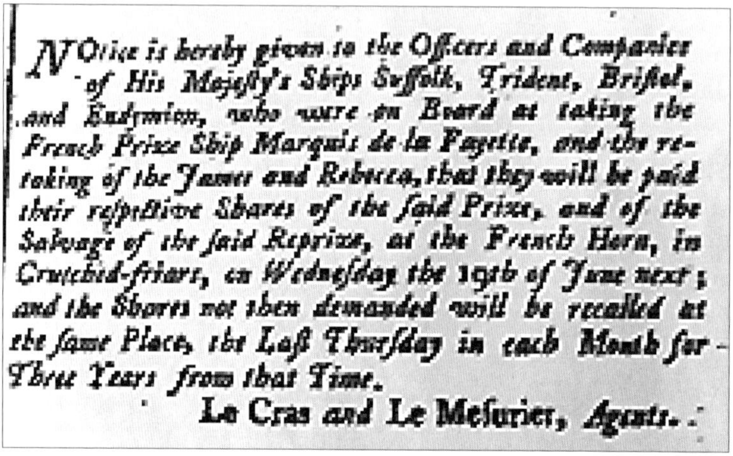

NOtice is hereby given to the Officers and Companies of His Majesty's Ships Suffolk, Trident, Bristol, and Endymion, who were on Board at taking the French Prize Ship Marquis de la Fayette, and the re-taking of the James and Rebecca, that they will be paid their respective Shares of the said Prize, and of the Salvage of the said Reprize, at the French Horn, in Crutched-friars, on Wednesday the 19th of June next; and the Shares not then demanded will be recalled at the same Place, the Last Thursday in each Month for Three Years from that Time.

Le Cras and Le Mesurier, *Agents.*

Notice from the Scots Magazine, *Edinburgh, May 1782*

Though Carteret's persistence in pestering Sandwich was understandable it did not help his case and only served to irritate him. Sandwich was commended for recognising and promoting Captain Cook, but he was a man with exceptional ability, Carteret was not and was expendable. His career is 'instructive in showing how the administration treated more ordinary men' no matter what he had achieved in the past it did not necessarily assure him of further employment.

Sandwich left office on 30 March 1782. Carteret immediately wrote a letter to the new First Lord Augustus Keppel; it is a draft and we do not know whether he sent it but it vividly expresses the pain he felt, to have been given such a summary dismissal,

> 'This uncivil and discouraging treatment was not only a mortification, but a great loss to me....I am totally ignorant to this moment what may have given room for such treatment or not being reimployed as I instantly made proffers of Service to Lord Sandwich'.

We learn from a letter written by Gower that Carteret had become an invalid due to his 'rheumatick complaints' (possibly a form of rheumatoid arthritis) and he asks Keppel if he could be considered for 'home duty'. He asks if he could be give command of the *Royal William*[6] or the Lieutenancy of Greenwich Hospital for he now has 'a large and young family to bring up'.

The gloom that descended on Carteret and his family must have been lightened in June 1782 when they learnt that Le Cras and Le Mesurier[7] would be paying the Officers and Companies of the *Suffolk, Trident, Endymion* and *Bristol* their shares of the prize money for the capture of the *Marquis de la Fayette* and the *Rebecca* and *James*. A notice in the *London Gazette* states that the money would be paid out at French Horn Yard, Crutched Friars on Wednesday 19 June. An original catalogue of the sale, with copious annotations and notes, belonged to Benjamin Franklin and it is now owned by the American Philosophical Society.

Panter and Co. of Mincing Lane acted as brokers and the sale was held at Garraway's Coffee-house, Exchange Alley, Cornhill. Bottled goods, medicines, wine, spirits and 113 boxes and chests of tea had been sold on 27 September. The rest of the cargo was sold over six days beginning on Tuesday 19 January 1782. The extent and variety of the cargo intended for military and civilian use meant that a different category was sold each day. These comprised uniforms for the army and ready-made garments, woollen fabrics, upholstery, East-India goods, haberdashery, arms and ammunition. The list of items give a fascinating glimpse into life of the time, from the 2,923 gross of pewter buttons with 'mark USA upon them', 503 pounds of white hair for wigs, 738 sailors hammocks, 32 umbrellas, 119 dozen ladies' fans, 4,694 feathers in six lots and 4,459 muskets mounted with bayonets and scabbards.

Carteret seems to have recovered by 1784, when Gower writes that he is pleased to hear that he and his wife are now in good health. But his prospects of preferment are dealt another blow that year when Lord North, First Lord of the Treasurer, refuses Earl Beauchamp's request that he champions Carteret's cause. Carteret does not give up and three years later, whilst on a visit to Jersey, he heard a rumour that there were preparations for war. He immediately wrote to the Admiralty that he was 'ready to Serve and obey their Commands' but receives no response. The following year the accounts show that building work was taking place at the Manor. Probably repairs to the damage done by the soldiers. On this trip he becomes ill, there is a bill for the surgeon's attendance and some medicine.

In 1782, Gower was appointed to the *Medea*. Although he had served successfully with Admiral Rodney in the West Indies and had been appointed Captain, he was dismayed by the heavy-handed and unco-operative attitude of the Admiralty. He wrote to Carteret that Sandwich:

> 'has made almost effectual sacrifice of me by forcing me to go to the East Indies, I wrote him a very strong letter stating my long services in Southern Climates, and the bad health I was subject to in them'

but it was made brutally plain that if he did not accept the commission to the *Medea* 'I must not expect to be employed again'.

It was in fact the beginning of a distinguished career for Gower. He accepted the posting to India and, on his return in 1785, asked Carteret if he would like him to enter his younger son Philip's name if 'Mrs Carteret and Yourself can make up your minds to let the Young one go so distant a Voyage'. In October 1785, Carteret writes apologising for the delay in replying to his letter but the unexpected death of his youngest child meant that he had to suddenly leave London for Southampton. He thanks him for his kind offer but declines as he does not think it is right 'to send young People to sea before they have acquired a good Education... I shall be obliged...to you to put him on your Books as a Servant' (entering a boy's name although he never came on board was a well-established practice). Philip does receive the education his father wanted and was a pupil at Winchester College from 1789 till 1792.

It would appear from comments made by a number of people that by 1790, Carteret was prematurely aged by the combined effects of illness and stress. He made his will that year appointing Le Cras, who had retired to Southampton, as an executor. He was to receive £20 and his sister Ann the £150 that he owed her. Only the immediate family, his wife and children are mentioned. His eldest son Samuel Silvester, born in 1775, inherited Trinity Manor. Two years later Carteret had a debilitating stroke, which caused loss of speech. Gower wrote to Mrs Carteret in August of that year that he had heard that it was his own bitter experience of the Navy that had made him decide 'that neither of his sons should be brought up either for the Navy or Army Professions'. However, he had made it plain that the decision rested with his sons and in 1792 Philip did enter the Navy, joining under the care of Gower in 1792 and sailing with him when he took Lord Macartney and his embassy to China. Gower was awarded a knighthood for this mission. Samuel Silvester served with the Royal Artillery from 1792 and was posted to the West Indies; he died there in 1796 (probably from yellow fever – there was a particularly virulent outbreak that year).

Carteret was retired with the rank of Rear Admiral on 29 April 1794 and even that was a matter of deep disappointment. His daughter Elizabeth believed that he 'would have had his proper Flag, & not been made a Superannuated Rear Admiral, had he not been confined to his Bed'.

Philip Carteret died on 21 July 1796 in his home in Southampton and was buried in the catacombs of All Saints' Church. If there was a memorial to Carteret in the nave or chancel of the church it was destroyed when the church was bombed and burnt out in 1940. The remains of the people buried in the catacombs were transferred to Hollybrook Cemetery on the outskirts of the city. Mary remained in the house at 76 High Street until 1802 but it too was destroyed in the bombing.

Postscript

In a letter dated 19 May 1797, Philip's son, later known as Philip Carteret Silvester, wrote to his mother:

> 'One of your former letters states, that you have sent a Box containing all my Fathers MSS, Journals Log Books &c to Mr Fitzhugh's; but would it not be better to take such sacred relicks (for I consider them as such) with you to place in the family Mansion'.

His mother agreed and the papers remained in the family until they were sold by Maggs Brothers of London in 1933. The Log, Journal and Abstract and other papers relating to the circumnavigation were bought by the Sir William Dixson of Sydney, New South Wales, and bequeathed by him to the Library of New South Wales, Australia. The remaining papers, notes and letters and correspondence of other members of the family were bought by the National Maritime Museum.

Philip and his sisters Elizabeth and Caroline cared passionately about their father's achievements and were incensed by the way the Navy had treated him. Elizabeth wrote shortly after his death that:

> 'It was ungenerous in the Admiralty not *fully* to reward a Man, whom had so highly deserved Reward, as having added to the fame of his Country and as a stimulus to others though he was then suffering from his exertions. He had taught the way to future Navigators and his Charts, although having very inadequate means to survey, have been found particularly correct.'

It is fortunate for posterity that his children took so much care in preserving the papers for it is only by reading Carteret's account of the 'true situation' that Hawkesworth's anodised version can be corrected.

Carteret was a perfectionist who found it difficult to accept anything that was second-best; the discrepancy between what he felt he deserved and what he actually got made him both deeply resentful and all the more determined to succeed. Harbouring grudges and assuming complicity where it did not exist led to errors of judgement. This combination of arrogance and intransigence inevitably brought him into conflict with authority whether it was a senior naval officer, Lemprière's regime in Jersey, the Admiralty or the Dutch. A letter from the Governor General of Batavia and the Council of the Netherlands Indies, written in October 1768, shows the Dutch were shocked by his behaviour, concluding that he did not

> 'deserve the least respect or indulgence, both because of his discourteous conduct in Celebes and his irreverent actions here...he has become consumed with arrogance'.

His inflexible and prickly temperament and frequent and vituperative complaints about the Admiralty's shortcomings also clouded his prospects at a time when competition for commissions in the Royal Navy was particularly intense. Carteret was sidelined whilst Gower, who was equally critical of the Admiralty, but confined it to private correspondence, went on to enjoy a distinguished career. He had realised that to prosper in a system which worked entirely by personal contacts it was the wordly-wise officer who used his social skills to network and seek out 'interests' who would be rewarded.

Fate was cruel to Carteret. At the very moment 'poor dull *Swallow*' was limping back to England, Captain Cook was en route to discovering Australia and New Zealand. On his return he was feted as a great British hero and assigned an unrivalled place in the history of exploration. Cook's achievement completely overshadowed Carteret's, despite the fact that he had pulled off an extraordinary feat of seamanship, rediscovered the legendary Solomon Islands and charted routes which were later followed by British ships making the voyage to China and Australia. Languishing back in Jersey on half-pay, his career in the Royal Navy faltered and his name was gradually forgotten.

Nearly 250 years after Carteret sighted and named a ring of small coral islands, 'all well cloathed with green Trees, and well inhabited', on the northern fringe of the Solomon Islands, the Carteret Islands are in the news again. Their inhabitants have become the world's first climate change refugees as rising sea levels have engulfed their islands, seawater floods have made the soils useless for growing crops and the fresh water supplies have been contaminated. Although the Islanders have done all they possibly can to contain and control the storm surges, some families have had to be evacuated and relocated to the 'mainland' – the island of Bougainville, 86 kilometres to the south-west which was discovered by fellow circumnavigator Bougainville. As well as the island of Bougainville his name was given to the South American climbing shrub *Bougainvillea* discovered by Philibert Commercon, a botanist on the *Boudeuse*. Thirteeen ships in the French Navy were named after him, one, a privateer, en route to St Malo, was captured by HMS *Scorpion;* the Captain was Philip Carteret Silvester. It is the final ironic twist to a story which began in July 1768 when Bougainville discovered the remains of the plaque that Carteret had nailed to a tree in English Cove the previous year, 'a very strange chance' which ultimately led to their surreal encounter in the Southern Atlantic.

It seems appropriate to leave the final assessment of Carteret's epic voyage to someone who was born in the part of the world which he so heroically tried to find. Sir Peter Henry Buck was born in New Zealand in 1877, the only son of William Buck and a Maori mother. The elders of her tribe gave him the name *Te Rangi Hiroa*. He went on to become an outstanding doctor, soldier, sportsman, Member of Parliament and anthropologist of the Maori and Polynesian people.

In his book *Explorers of the Pacific* published in 1953 he wrote,

> 'Though Carteret added little to Polynesian discovery his voyage was one of the pluckiest in history. Not only should the *Swallow* have been relegated to the scrap heap instead of being sent out on an expedition, the Admiralty had refused to supply Carteret with an anvil and other equipment for repairs.The story of how he circumnavigated the world in a leaking tub and kept her afloat for 2 years and 7 months will ever remain a record of endurance, courage and skill.'

NOTES

Introduction

1 The *Boudeuse* was launched on 25 March 1766 from the Indret Yard in Nantes. She was a 580-ton ship carying 26 x 12 pounders and a complement of 214 men. She played an active role in both the American Revolutionary Wars and the French Revolutionary Wars.

2 The *Swallow* was launched on 14 December 1745 from Bird's Yard in Rotherhithe. She was a 278-ton snow-rigged sloop carrying 14 x 4 pounders and 14 swivel guns. Her complement of men was 110. In 1755 she was re-rigged as a ship-rigged sloop, which would have meant changing her from a two masted to a three-masted vessel. She was sold out of service in 1769

Chapter 1: 'To be Englisched'

1 In 1822 he added his mother's surname to his own and, on the death of her brother, Sir John Silvester, succeeded to the baronetcy thus becoming Sir Philip Carteret Silvester.

2 George Carteret (1609-1680) dropped the 'de' from his surname when he joined the English navy. He was knighted by Charles II in 1649 following his proclaimation as King in Jersey earlier that year.

3 Grampus was derived from the Latin terms for great fish and over the centuries was applied to many species including killer whales (*orcinus orca*).

4 Amias or Amice de Carteret served as Bailiff of Guernsey between 1601 until his death in 1631. He also served as Lieutenant-Governor to Sir Thomas Leighton and then to Lord George Carew.

5 The *Salisbury*, a 50-gun fourth rate ship-of-the-line was built by Philopmmon Ewer of East Cowes on the Isle of Wight. She was launched on 29 January 1746 and was armed with 22 x 24 pounders, 22 x 12 pounders and 6 x 6pounders. She carried a complement of 300 men.

6 The *Monmouth*, was originally built as a 68-gun, third rate ship-of-the–line by Phineas Pett II at Chatham in 1667. She was rebuilt in 1700, 1718 and 1742 by which time she was a 70-gun third rate ship-of-the-line carrying 26 x 24 pounder cannon, 2 6 x 12 pounders and 18 x 6 pounders.

7 The *St Albans* was a 60-gun fourth rate ship-of-the-line built at Deptford. She was launched on 23 February 1747.

8 HMS *Augusta* was a 60-gun fourthrate ship-of-the-line built at Deptford. She was launched on 1 July 1736.

9 The *Vanguard* was a 70-gun third rate ship-of-the-line built by Philip Ewer at his yard in East Cowes on the Isle of Wight. She was launched on 16 April 1648.

10 The *Dunkirk* was a 60-gun fourth rate ship-of-the-line built at Woolwich Dockyard. She was launched on 22 July 1754.

11 The *Guernsey* was launched as a 50-gun fourth rate ship-of-the-line at Blackwall on the Thames in 1696. She was rebuilt and relaunched at Woolwich in 1717 and then in 1737 she was ordered to be taken to pieces and rebuilt at Chatham. Once this was done she was relaunched on 11 August 1740 and she remained on active service until she was hulked in 1769.

Chapter 2: 'The Key to the Pacific Ocean'

1 The *America* was a 60-gun fourth rate ship-of-the-line built by Wells and Stanton at Rotherhithe. She was launched on 21 May 1757.
2 The *Fame* was a 74-gun third rate ship-of-the-line built by Henry Bird at Deptford and launched in January 1759.
3 *Achilles*, (60) and the *Dorsetshire* (70)
4 The Battle of Restigouche, July 1759.
5 The *Wager* was a small East India man bought into the Navy to serve as a 22-gun sixth rate storeship in November 1739 to serve in Anson's fleet which was to circumnavigate the world in 1740. She was wrecked on the coast of Chile on 14 May 1741.
6 *Aigle* was a 300-ton frigate which carried a crew of about 300
7 The *Dolphin* was a 24-gun sixth rate frigate launched from the Woolwich Dockyard in May 1751.
8 The *Tamar* was a 16-gun ship sloop launched from Snook's yard in Saltash Cornwall in January 1758.
9 Port Famine, now known as Puerto del Hambro or Ciudad del Rey Don Felipe, Chile, lies on the north shore of the Strait of Magellan in Buena Bay.
10 The French circumnavigator Louis Antoine de Bougainville (1729-1811) had already formally claimed the islands, which the French called Les Iles Malouines, in April 1764 and the harbour Byron named Port Egmont was already known as Port de la Croisade.
11 Port Desire is now known as Puerto Deseado in the Argentinian province of Santa Cruz.
12 The *Florida* was a merchantman bought into the Navy in August 1764
13 Port Louis is a small settlement on Berkeley Sound, East Falkland.
14 Lat: 53° 30' 37" S Long: 72° 35' 34" W
15 The bower anchor was situated on the ship's bow and was one of the main anchors.
16 Scurvy grass was the name given to a wide variety of plants rich in vitamin C.
17 Batavia was renamed Jakarta in 1942 during the Japanese occupation of Indonesia.
18 General Henry Seymour-Conway was appointed Governor of Jersey in October 1772
19 Samuel Wallis passed his lieutenant's examination in October 1748 and enjoyed the patronage of Vice-Admiral Edward Boscawen through whom he was appointed Master and Commander in June 1756 and made Post-Captain the following April.

Chapter 3: Poor dull *Swallow*

1 She was launched by Henry Bird from his yard at Rotherhithe in December 1745. She had an additional mast added in 1755 to become rated as a ship-sloop.
2 *Prince Frederick* was rebuilt at Deptford and relaunched in March 1740; by 1764 she had been hulked and was then a storeship.
3 The *Prince of Orange*, third rate 70-gun ship-of-the-line launched from the Deptford Dockyard in September 1739.
4 Junk was the name given to the old cordage which was used for tying sails and making repairs and Carteret wrote had uses too many to enumerate.
5 Bahía Upright lies just to the south of Cabo Upright and to the west of Estero Córdova.
6 Celebes is now known as Sulawesi. It is one of the Indonesian Great Sunda Islands. In the 18th century it was controlled by the Dutch East India Company.

Chapter 6: 'Merittable but unnoticed Voyage'

1 A cat was a style of very strongly built sailing collier designed to carry 500-600 tons of coal. They were very common throughout the North Sea area.
2 The vessel in question was the 368-ton *Earl of Pembroke* built by Thomas Fishburn in Whitby.
3 The *Cherokee* was a 177-ton six-gun armed ship bought into the Royal Navy in September 1774. In 1777 she was renamed the Despatch and used as an armed transport.

Chapter 7: 'Hawkesworth has brewed it'

1 The *Endymion* was a 44-gun fifth rate ship launched by Greaves of Limehouse in 1779.
2 The *Flamborough* was a 20-gun sixth rate ship launched by Batson of Limehouse in May 1756. It was sold out of the Navy in 1772.
3 Before he joined the Royal Navy, Pascal had been master of the *Industrious Bee*, owned by Guernseyman Nicholas Dobrée. Pascal had taken her to Virginia from whence he had brought back an 11-year-old slave called Olaudah Equiano (c.1745-97). Equiano's auto-biography, The Interesting Narrative of the Life of Olaudah Equiano or Gustavus Vasa, the African caused a sensation when it was published in 1789.

Chapter 8: That neglected and gallant officer

1 The *Levant* was a 28-gun frigate launched by Adams at his yard at Beaulieu, Hampshire in July 1758.
2 The *Sandwich* was a second rate 98-gun ship-of-the-line originally built as a 90-gun ship at the Chatham Dockyard in 1756.
3 The *Pomona* a sixth rate 28-gun frigate was launched from the Raymond yard in Southampton in September 1778.
4 John Barry (1745-1803) did much to organise the new American Navy and following Independence was appointed Senior Captain.
5 The *Cambridge* was a 80-gun third rate ship-of-the-line launched from the Deptford Dockyard in October 1755. She had been hulked between 1777 and 1782 and used as a prison ship for captured enemy seamen in Plymouth.
6 The *Royal William* was originally built as a 100-gun first rate man-of-war in 1719 in Portsmouth Dockyard. She was cut down to an 84 gun second rate ship in 1756.
7 Guernseyman Paul Le Mesurier (1755–1805) joined Le Cras in 1776 when he married his niece Margaret Roberdeau. He was also an underwriter at Lloyds, shipowner, a director of the East India Company and Lord Mayor of London (1793-4). His exceptionally fine court coat is in the National Trust of Guernsey's Folk and Costume Museum.

REFERENCES

Two short accounts of Carteret's life have been published:
A Biographical Dictionary of Jersey, G R Balleine, La Haule Books, 1993, pp.112-4
Rear-Admiral Philippe de Carteret, A C Saunders, *Société Jersiaise Bulletin*, X1 1931, pp.315-25

Introduction

A voyage round the World. Performed...in the years 1766-9, L A de Bougainville, French edition published 1771, English translation, London 1772

Extracts from the *Gazette de France*, 1768 as seen by Bougainville in January 1769 at the Cape of Good Hope are quoted in:

Carteret's Voyage round the world 1766-9, edited Helen Wallis, 2 vols. Published for the Hakluyt Society, Cambridge University Press 1965

Chapter 1: 'To be Englisched'

36 years of a seafaring life, John Bechervaise, 1839, pp.10-11

Carteret's Memorandum of Service 1747-56 quoted by Helen Wallis, op.cit. Vol 2, p.279

A True and Impartiall Journal of a Voyage to the South Seas and Round the Globe in His Majesty's ship the Centurion, 1745, Pascoe Thomas

Log of the Centurion. *Based on the original papers of Captain Philip Saumarez on board HMS* Centurion, *Lord Anson's flagship during his circumnavigation 1740-44*, by Leo Heaps, New York, Macmillan, 1973

The Wager Disaster: Mayhem, Mutiny and Murder in the South Seas. Admiral C.H.Layman, Uniform Press, 2015

Voltaire quoted in *The Trial of the Cannibal Dog; the remarkable story of Captain Cook's encounters in the South Seas*, Anne Salmond, paperback reprint, Penguin Books New Zealand, 2004, p.11

Inventory of Trinity Manor, 1696, Jersey Archive L/C/93/B/53

Family debts *Accounts of Philippe Carteret with Charles Poingdestre and Pierre Mauger his procurers 1761-1815* L/C/66/B4/43

Chapter 2: **The Key to the Pacific Ocean**

An Account of the Voyages undertaken by the order of his present Majesty for making Discoveries in the Southern Hemphishere, and successively performed by Commodore Byron, Captain Wallis, Captain Carteret and Captain Cook, John Hawkesworth, 3 vols.1773

The History of a Voyage to the Malouine Islands made in 1763 and 1764, Antoine Joseph Pernetty, London 1771.

Chapter 3: Poor dull *Swallow*

Muster Book of the Swallow Public Record Office ADM.36/7511

The Discovery of Tahiti. A Journal of the second voyage of HMS Dolphin round the world under the command of Captain Wallis, George Robertson ed.Hugh Carrington, Hakluyt Society, Ser.11.No.98.London 1948

Chapter 4: Abandoned

'Oro, Salmond, op.cit.p.45

William Dampier - *Australia Bound. The Story of West Country Connections*, Martyn Brown. Ex Libris Press, 1988, pp.26-7

Chapter 5: Homeward Bound

Resolutions of the Council of Macassar and the Council of the Netherlands Indies at Batavia and other Dutch records, 18 December 1767-20 October 1768 Rijksarchief, quoted by Helen Wallis, *op.cit*.

Chapter 6: 'Merittable but unnoticed Voyage'

Tahiti poem - Salmond, *op.cit*.p27

An account of Bougainville's stay in Tahiti in April 1768 can be found in *L'Art des voyages Français en Polynésie 1768–1846*. Christine A. Hemming. Somogy Éditions d'Art, Paris, 2013. Text is in French and English

Chapter 7: 'Hawkesworth has brewed it'

Journal de Daniel Messervy 1769-1772, Daniel Messervy, Société Jersiaise (publication no.11), 1896

Foreword by Jacob, 8th Earl of Radnor to *The French Hospital in England; its Huguenot History and Collections*, Tessa Murdoch, John Adamson, 2009.

Also contains information and portraits of Isaac Gosset, Francois Duroure and Dr. Matthew Maty.

Jersey merchants in London - A *People of the Sea. The Maritime History of the Channel Islands.* edt. A G Jamieson, Methuen, 1986, p.313

Gossets - National Portrait Gallery. *British picture framemakers, 1630-1950*. www.npg.org.uk

A Family of Modellers in Wax, Mary H.Gosset. Publications of the Huguenot Society.Vol.3. 1892.pp.540

Silvester's house and garden - *Loddiges of Hackney the largest hothouse in the world*, David Solman, Hackney Society Publication,1995

Spurstowe's House and Silvester's Garden, Isobel Watson, The Hackney Terrier 1991/2, Hackney Archives Department

Pascal's will - *Olaudah Equiano; An African slave in Guernsey*, Brycchan Carey,The Guernsey Society, Summer 2003

Walpole, Wallis, *op.cit* p.466

Boswell ibid p.472

Burney ibid p.475

Chapter 8: That neglected and gallant officer

Carteret's Diary National Maritime Museum Archive 35 MS.0081.CAR/3

Carteret's account whilst Captain of *Endymion* 1 September 1780 - 31 August 1781 Public Record Office, ADM 51/296

Sale of contents of Trinity Manor Jersey Archive. Account of Philippe Carteret with Charles Poingdestre 1779-92, L/F/101/A/5

Account of Richard de Carteret with James Hemery agent for the ship *Venus 1774*. Jersey Archive, L/C/47/A/579

The Insatiable Earl; A Life of John Montagu, Fourth Earl of Sandwich, N A M Rodger, Harper Collins, 1993

Sale catalogue of prize cargo of the Marquis de la Fayette, 1781-2. American Philosophical Society, Mss.347.7.P19

Carteret's will. Public Record Office PROB 11/1278

ACKNOWLEDGEMENTS

I would like to thank Doug Ford and Jersey Heritage for asking me to tell the story of this 'neglected and gallant' Jerseyman. Doug's incomporable knowledge of all things maritime was invaluable. Huge thanks also to the publisher, Roger Jones of Seaflower Books, for doing such a brilliant job of editing and improving the manuscript. Thanks also to Val Nelson and Louise Downey from Jersey Heritage for their patience and hard work. The contribution made by Anna Baghiani, Marie-Louise-Backhurst, John Haley and Jersey Archive was much appreciated. A big thank you to Ned Malet de Carteret for drawing attention to plight of the Carteret Islanders.

My thanks to the Halkluyt Society for granting me permission to reproduce sections of text from the two volumes of their publication *Carteret's Voyage Round the World 1766-69* edited by Helen Wallis, Cambridge University Press, 1965.

Also Penguin (New Zealand) for reproducing quotations from Anne Salmond's book *The Trial of the Cannibal Dog The remarkable story of Captain Cook's Encounter in the South Seas*, 2004. Jacob, 8th Earl of Radnor for permission to quote from his foreword to *The French Hospital in England*, Tessa Murdoch, John Adamson, 2007, and the State Library of New South Wales, Australia.

Ilustrations from Doug Ford, Jersey Heritage/Societe Jersiaise Collection, National Maritime Museum, Greenwich, London, National Library of Australia.

The Carteret Islands Today

by Ned Malet de Carteret

The Carteret Islands in the Pacific Ocean stand 86 kilometres north east of Bougainville, an autonomous island ceded from Papua New Guinea. They were discovered in 1767 by Captain Philip Carteret RN (1733-1796). He was on his second circumnavigation of the globe in HMS Swallow. Carteret later became a Rear Admiral and Seigneur of Trinity in Jersey, dying in Southampton.

Bougainville Island is the main island of the Autonomous Region of Bougainville of Papua New Guinea. The population of the province is approximately 175,000 which includes the adjacent island of Buka and assorted outlying islands including the Carterets (called Tuluun by the inhabitants). The group of seven Carteret Islands include the principal island of Han, they are coral reefs standing some 1.5 metres above the current sea level.

The 2,700 residents, who are Halia speaking, came to the Islands some 400 years ago from the neighbouring Baku Island. The societies are matriarchal. Oral tradition has that the islands have been inhabited for over 1,000 years by Polynesians. The Islanders survive in the main on taros, greens, breadfruit, coconuts and fishing. A supply boat comes once a year from Bougainville bringing other supplies and rice. The population has grown as people have emigrated from Bougainville during the bitter Civil War of the 1980/90s.

The Islands rest on the world's largest tectonic plate – the Pacific Plate. King Tides prevail in the month of December. In 1984 Huene Island was permanently divided in two by the sea.

The Carteret Islanders are set to become the World's first environmental refugees, as the Islands are predicted to sink under rising sea levels by 2040/50. Since 2006 the Islands' chiefs have appointed Tuele Peisa, an NGO based in Bougainville, with the task of re-locating Islanders to Bougainville and the organisation is headed up by Ursula Rakova. To date through gifts by various charitable organisations, only ten families – some 67 residents have been re-located to Tinputz and Woroav on 30 hectares of land donated by the Catholic Church. The families subsist by growing cacao.

In 2018 I came into contact with Ursula Rakova and brought the plight of the Islands and their people to the attention of Channel Island residents. A small amount of monies has been raised to help them. I fear that the majority of Carteret Islanders will not leave their homes until the very last moment.